HANDY
PET CARE
GUIDES

Choosing &
Looking After Your

Horse

This is a **FLAME TREE** book
First published in 2014

Publisher and Creative Director: Nick Wells
Senior Project Editor: Catherine Taylor
Picture Research: Victoria Lyle, Gemma Walters
Art Director: Mike Spender
Illustrator: Ann Biggs
Copy Editor: Emily Anderson
Indexer: Helen Snaith

Special thanks to: Esme Chapman, Emma Chafer, Tamsin Pickeral.

FLAME TREE PUBLISHING
Crabtree Hall, Crabtree Lane
Fulham, London SW6 6TY
United Kingdom

www.flametreepublishing.com

First published 2014

14 16 18 17 15
1 3 5 7 9 10 8 6 4 2

A CIP record for this book is available from the British Library upon request.

ISBN 978-1-78361-228-4

Printed in Singapore

All photographs are courtesy of **Bob Langrish** except: **Corbis:** Bo Zaunders 167.
Shutterstock: Jackiso 30; Catherine311 33; Virtuelle 170; Terry Alexander 109;
Cheryl Ann Quigley 198; Gabriel Moisa 180.

HANDY
PET CARE
GUIDES

Choosing &
Looking After Your

Horse

PIPPA ROOME & CATHERINE AUSTEN

**FLAME TREE
PUBLISHING**

Contents

Caring for & Riding Your Horse . . 118

Introduction

Horses and ponies have made firm companions for millions of years, from creatures of burden enriching the lives of human beings through transport and agricultural means to their more familiar role in sport and leisure. In this guide, discover comprehensive information about our equine friends, how to choose and take good care of your horse and how to enjoy rewarding riding and competing.

With practical information on the basic principles of horse riding to grooming and how to tack up your horse, *Choosing & Looking After Your Horse* is ideal for those considering owning a horse for the first time as well as experienced horse owners who may be considering competing with their horse. The guide contains useful information on how to care for your horse and deal with the numerous ailments that can afflict him. Key aspects of horse ownership are covered, from buying the correct equipment to ensuring a suitable environment is achieved.

Information on the types of horses and ponies out there, from polo pony to hack, cob and warmblood, along with detailed diagrams and in-depth descriptions of the anatomy, senses and distinguishing features of the horse will allow the reader to know their animal from mane to hoof. Equine instinct and behaviour will be brought to life as the book guides you through the many, varying aspects of a horse's psychological make-up, giving you invaluable advice on how best to deal with these intelligent and sensitive creatures.

Choosing & Looking After Your Horse is an indispensable guide for all horse lovers – from first time owners to successive generations of horse enthusiasts – there is something for everyone.

How
Horses
work

Types of Horses and Ponies

'Types' of horses are not breeds, but usually a group of breeds that share similar characteristics or are used for a particular activity such as polo or hunting. They do not have a breed registry, and may either be one of a certain number of different registered breeds, or horses of mixed and indifferent breeding that are alike in appearance, behaviour or use. Polo ponies, cobs, hacks, hunters, draught horses, gaited horses – all are examples of 'types' of horse.

Polo Pony

All horses used to play the sport of polo are referred to as 'ponies', although most of them will be quite a bit bigger than the official maximum height of a pony (14.2 hands (hh), or 147 cm/57 in). Most polo ponies measure between 15 hh and 16 hh, and are usually Thoroughbreds. Many ex-racehorses find a second career in polo, but there are also studs which purpose-breed polo ponies, particularly in Argentina. There the ponies may be a combination of Thoroughbred blood and the native Criollo breed. Polo ponies need to be fast, agile and quick-thinking – and, due to the rough nature of the sport, brave. They are competed with hogged (shaven) manes.

► The polo pony business is a big money game, and quality ponies with tenacity and speed sell for vast sums of money.

Riding Pony

The term 'riding pony' is usually used to refer to show ponies, originally developed in the United Kingdom, but now found worldwide. Ranging in height from about 12 hh to 14.2 hh, they are fine, elegant creatures that more resemble small horses than traditional ponies. They are usually a mix of either Thoroughbred or Arab blood with Welsh, and developed after the Second World War when small Thoroughbreds and Arabs were turned out on the Welsh hills to improve the stock. There are three main types: the show pony, which looks like a miniature show hack or Thoroughbred; the show hunter pony, which is just as elegant, but stockier and able to carry a little more weight; and the working hunter pony, which has more substance and is more 'workmanlike' than the other two types.

Hunter

'Hunters' can either be show hunters, or 'working' hunters, i.e. those whose job it is to go hunting, termed in the United States a 'field hunter'. Show hunters in the United States are usually judged on how well they perform over a course of fences; show hunters in the United Kingdom are usually exhibited on the flat. Turnout, attitude, movement and conformation are important. In the United Kingdom, show hunter classes are divided into lightweight, middleweight and heavyweight sections, and are won by quality animals that demonstrate substance, manners and elegance.

◄ Cobs are distinctively heavy through their frame and generally have the most wonderful, calm temperaments.

► Hunters vary considerably in stamp and type, but should always have correct conformation and good paces.

'Field' hunters must have the stamina, manners, jumping ability, boldness and speed to carry their riders over a variety of terrain for several hours at a time. They come in an infinite variety of shapes and sizes, but are united by possessing the characteristics listed above.

Hack

Hacks are one of the most elegant members of the showing community, and should have superb movement, manners and conformation. They are primarily Thoroughbreds, and classes are divided into small hacks (up to 15 hh) and large hacks (up to 15.3 hh). Disobedience and misbehaviour are severely punished in hack classes – they are supposed to perform an advanced show smoothly, calmly and obediently. The type originally developed from the smart riding horses that ladies and gentlemen used to parade around London's Hyde Park in the nineteenth century in order to 'be seen'.

Cob

'Cobs' are small, stocky horses with compact bodies, short legs and steady dispositions. They are usually of unknown or mixed breeding; perhaps an Irish Draught horse crossed with a hunter mare with a little Thoroughbred blood. They are different from Welsh Cobs, which are a separate breed. It is said that the classic show cob has 'the head of a lady and the backside of a cook'. Show cobs in the United Kingdom are divided into three classes: lightweight cobs, heavyweight cobs and maxi-cobs.

Warmblood

'Warmblood' is a generic term used to describe a group of sport horses, originally developed in Europe, that resulted from a cross between coldbloods (draught horses) and hotbloods (Arabs and Thoroughbreds).

▶ The Hack is an elegant show horse, and should have impeccable manners as well as superb conformation and movement.

Particularly used in show jumping and dressage due to their good movement and trainable temperaments, there are a number of different types, such as Swedish Warmblood, Dutch Warmblood, Trakehner, Danish Warmblood, Selle Français, Hanoverian and Holsteiner. Each has slight variations, but are similar types. They have become increasingly popular in the eventing world since more emphasis was placed on the dressage phase, but many event riders still prefer the Thoroughbred's bravery. The warmbloods' studbooks are carefully regulated, and stock are performance-tested, with the emphasis placed on rideability and temperament.

Draught Horse

These are large, heavy horses originally used for pulling agricultural machinery and for farm work, such as Shires, Clydesdales, Percherons and Suffolk Punches. Although rarely used for their traditional occupations nowadays, the breeds are still preserved, through the show ring and for exhibitions. Often they are crossed with lighter breeds, such as the Thoroughbred, to produce sport horses and riding animals. They have been developed for strength, docility, patience and stamina, with muscular builds. Their conformation tends to be more upright through the shoulder than most riding horses, to equip them better for pulling carts and machinery.

Palomino Horses

Palomino is a colour, not strictly a type, but is often seen as one and there are separate showing classes for them. Any breed or type can be registered as palomino providing it has a golden-coloured coat and white mane or tail. Some breeds that have palomino representatives are the American Saddlebred, Tennessee Walking Horse, Morgan and Quarter Horse. The colour is fairly rare in the Thoroughbred, but does in fact occur and is recognized by the Jockey Club (the breed registry for thoroughbred horses in the US, Canada and Puerto Rico).

▶ Palomino horses are generally greatly sought after due to their appealing colour, and are particularly popular in America.

Mountain and Moorland

The term 'mountain and moorland' is used to describe the breeds of pony native to the British Isles. Shetlands, Exmoors, Dartmoors, and Welsh Sections A and B ponies are called the small breeds, whereas Highlands, Connemaras, Dales, Fells, New Forests and Welsh Sections C and D ponies are the large breeds. They are shown in their native state, untrimmed with unpulled and unplaited manes. They are hardy and designed to survive in relatively poor grazing areas, and often become fat and 'overtopped' unless their nutritional intake is carefully controlled.

Gaited Horses

This is the collective term for horses that perform the smooth, four-beat intermediate gaits known as 'ambling'. Ambling is usually faster than a walk, but slower than a canter. There are two basic types:

lateral, where the front and hind feet on the same side move in sequence; and diagonal, where the front and hind feet on opposite sides move in sequence. Examples of gaited horses include the American Saddlebred, the Paso Fino, the Tennessee Walking Horse, the Racking, some Saddlebreds and the Icelandic horse. The latter's four-beat gait is known as the 'tolt', and is a surprisingly comfortable way to cover long distances over rocky terrain.

◀ Draught breeds are termed 'coldbloods', and are defined by their equable temperaments.

▶ In the show ring mountain and moorland ponies should be presented with their mane and tail in their naturally long state.

Anatomy and Appearance

Physically, horses and ponies vary as much as, if not more than, humans. The different breeds and types all have their own characteristics. Although all horses may look like similar large, four-legged animals to the untrained observer, to the expert it is obvious that each equine is an individual, with its own shape, colour and personality. Biologically, the horse is a complex system. Horses have more than 200 bones, as well as a well-developed muscular system and numerous essential organs.

Points, Skeleton and Organs

Before we consider the points, skeleton and organs of a horse, we should look at the straightforward aspects of height and weight.

Horses are measured at the highest point of the withers, the bony part at the base of the neck. Traditionally, horses are measured in hands, each hand being 10 cm (4 in). The common abbreviation for this is 'hh' (hands high), so a horse might be described as 15.2 hh (15 hands and 2 in). Ponies measure 14.2 hh or less. More recently, equines have started to be measured in centimetres for competitions, so, for example, some 12.2 hh classes have been replaced by 128-cm classes.

A 16.2 hh horse weighs, on average, around 600 kg (94 stones 7 pounds), depending on its type and condition.

Points of the Horse

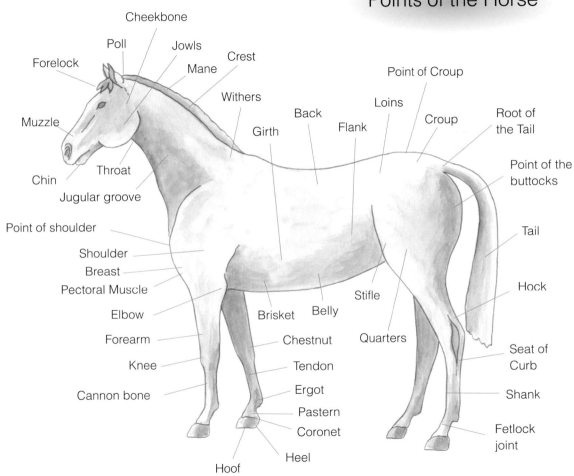

Cheekbone
Poll
Jowls
Crest
Forelock
Mane
Muzzle
Withers
Back
Flank
Loins
Point of Croup
Croup
Root of the Tail
Girth
Throat
Chin
Jugular groove
Point of the buttocks
Point of shoulder
Shoulder
Breast
Pectoral Muscle
Tail
Elbow
Brisket
Belly
Stifle
Hock
Forearm
Chestnut
Quarters
Knee
Tendon
Cannon bone
Ergot
Pastern
Coronet
Seat of Curb
Shank
Heel
Hoof
Fetlock joint

Points of the Horse

These are the terms used to describe certain specific external parts of the horse. The 'points' of the horse include the muzzle, poll, withers, stifle, hock, girth, quarters and tail, among others. They have several practical applications, such as in telling a vet exactly where a horse is injured or judging conformation. If used in relation to describing colour, the points of the horse refer to the mane, tail, muzzle, tips of the ears and lower legs.

Skeleton

The horse's skeleton has two separate parts, the axial and appendicular skeletons.

The **axial** skeleton is the skull, backbone and ribcage (including the sternum and the ribs). It protects vital organs such as the brain, spinal cord, heart and lungs, and gives the body shape. The backbone does not run all the way along the top of the horse. Behind the horse's poll it curves downwards towards the underside of the neck. As the shape of the crest of the neck is determined by muscle, not bone, it can be changed by exercise.

The **appendicular** skeleton consists of the bones of the horse's legs, and the associated bones in the shoulders and hindquarters.

The horse's muscles attach to the skeleton and work with ligaments and tendons to allow the animal to move.

◄ The skeleton of a fine horse is barely covered by the muscles, nerves and skin.

Skeleton of the Horse

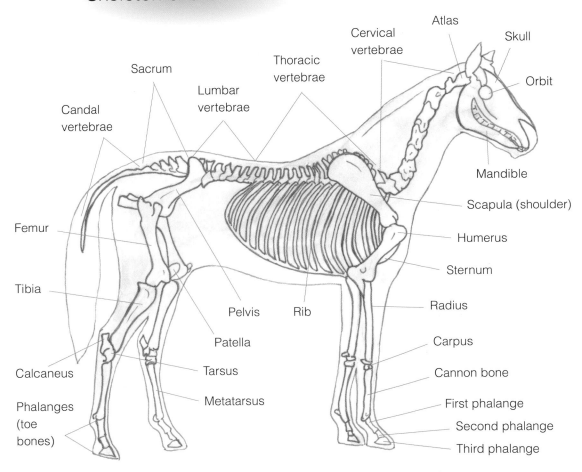

Atlas

Cervical
vertebrae

Skull

Thoracic
vertebrae

Orbit

Sacrum

Lumbar
vertebrae

Candal
vertebrae

Mandible

Scapula (shoulder)

Femur

Humerus

Sternum

Tibia

Radius

Pelvis

Rib

Patella

Carpus

Calcaneus

Tarsus

Cannon bone

Metatarsus

First phalange

Phalanges
(toe
bones)

Second phalange

Third phalange

Principal Organs and Systems

The horse's **heart** sits slightly to the left side of its chest and pumps blood around the body. Gaseous exchange, which sends oxygen around the body in the blood and returns carbon dioxide to the lungs to be breathed out, takes place in the lungs.

The horse's food passes from the mouth, down the oesophagus and into the stomach. The muscle at the entrance to the stomach, the cardiac sphincter, is like a one-way street: food cannot pass back through it, so horses cannot vomit.

Digestion begins in the stomach. The food gradually passes into the small intestine, which is around 22 m long, then into the shorter large intestine. As food travels along the intestines, it is broken down and nutrients are absorbed through the walls into the blood. By the time the food reaches the rectum, only waste is left, which leaves the horse's body as droppings through the anus.

Approximately 65 per cent of the horse's body consists of water. The horse has two kidneys, which filter the blood and send the waste and excess water to the bladder, where it is held until the horse urinates.

The horse also has a complex nervous system, a reproductive system, an endocrine system for releasing hormones and a lymphatic system, which drains excess fluid and helps the body to fight infection.

◄ The digestive system, heart and nervous system combine to create a finely tuned and powerful creature in a thoroughbred horse,

Digestive System of the Horse

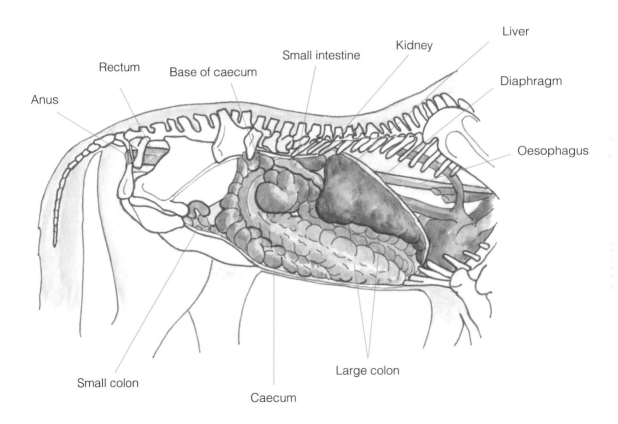

Teeth and Age

Milk and Permanent Teeth

Foals have a full set of milk teeth, some of which may be present at birth. The milk teeth continue to develop until the horse is around a year old. From the age of two and a half, the horse sheds its milk teeth and the permanent teeth replace them.

How Many Teeth?

Adult horses usually have 12 incisors, 12 premolars and 12 molars. Incisors are the biting teeth at the front of the mouth, while the premolars and molars are used for chewing and are at the back.

In addition, male horses (stallions or geldings, which are castrated males) generally have four canines (or tushes) in the 'interdental space' between the incisors and the premolars. Females (mares) do not usually have canines and, if they do, they are likely to be small. So most adult geldings and stallions have 40 teeth, while mares have 36.

Some horses also have one or more wolf teeth. These sit in front of the second premolar (the first tooth behind the interdental space) and are the remnants of the old defunct first premolar. Sometimes the wolf teeth cause pain or problems with the bit and are removed.

◄ The first of the temporary foal teeth to erupt are the two central incisors on the top and bottom jaw, as seen.

► Detailed diagram of the teeth in a horse's skull.

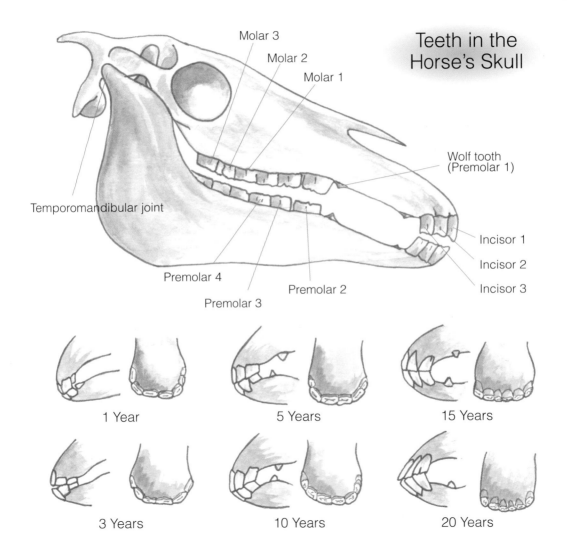

Teeth in the Horse's Skull

Molar 3

Molar 2

Molar 1

Wolf tooth (Premolar 1)

Temporomandibular joint

Incisor 1

Incisor 2

Incisor 3

Premolar 4

Premolar 2

Premolar 3

1 Year

5 Years

15 Years

3 Years

10 Years

20 Years

Ageing

An experienced person can age younger horses with some accuracy. After the age of eight there are clues, but even an expert can be 5 to 10 years out in their estimation. The development of the incisors is the clearest ageing tool.

The middle two incisors on each jaw are the central incisors. The temporary centrals are the first milk teeth to come out, at two-and-a-half years, and by three the horse will have its full permanent centrals. At three and a half, the next two teeth back on each jaw on each side, the temporary lateral incisors, come out, replaced by the age of four by their permanent equivalents.

At four and a half, the horse sheds the temporary corner incisors, the furthest back of these front teeth. By the age of five, their permanent replacements are fully grown. Males generally grow their tushes between the ages of four and five.

At seven, a hook appears on the corner incisors of the top jaw, hanging over the top of the lower corner incisors. This will remain for around a year. Another hook can appear later in life, often at around 13, which is generally permanent. As the horse ages, the teeth slope forwards more and appear longer.

Galvayne's Groove This develops down the outside of the upper corner incisors. The groove usually appears at around the age of 10, will be halfway down the tooth at 15 and stretches to the bottom at 20. By the age of 25, the groove will have disappeared from the top half of the tooth and at 30 it will have gone altogether.

Tables

The teeth wear down with use, and more is pushed up through the gum. The top surface of the lower incisors, the 'tables', can be used to help with ageing, as a different cross-section is exposed.

► Galvayne's groove appears as a dark line running vertically down the corner incisor. On this fifteen-year old horse the groove can be seen to have extended over halfway down the tooth.

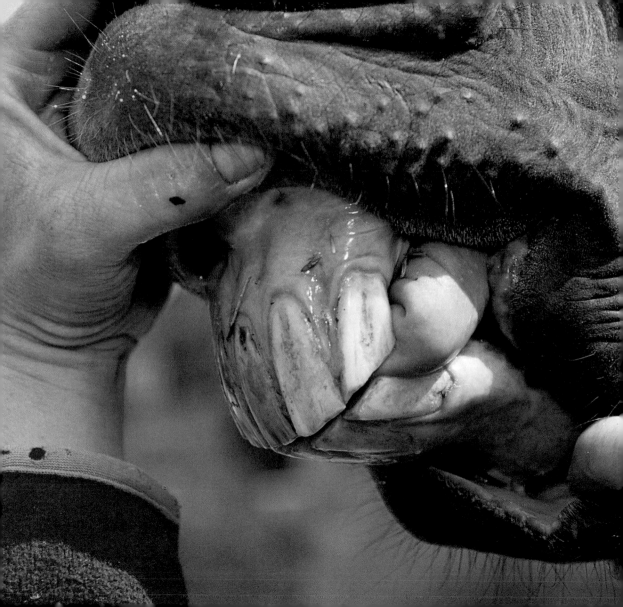

In the younger horse, a large dark hole shows in the centre of the table, called the 'infundibulum'. This gets smaller with age until it disappears completely. As the infundibulum shrinks, a black mark between it and the front of the teeth grows. This is the 'dental star'.

The central incisors show these changes first, then the laterals, and next the corner incisors. By the time the horse is eight years old, the infundibulum is likely to be nearly gone or have disappeared completely, with the dental star much in evidence. With continuing wear, the dental star becomes a dot in the middle of the tooth.

With increasing age, the tables also become more triangular.

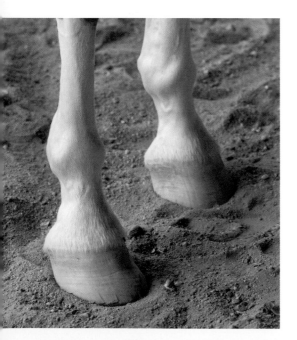

Structure of the Foot

External parts

The outside of the horse's foot, which can be seen when the foot is on the ground, is called the 'hoof wall'. When the foot is lifted, the sole and frog underneath are visible. The wall grows continuously, taking about a year to regenerate from top to bottom. The domesticated horse wears the foot down faster than happens in the wild, which is why most horses wear metal shoes. A farrier will trim the foot and replace the shoes approximately every six weeks.

◄ The foot of a horse grows continuously, taking almost a year to create a new foot from top to bottom.

► Detailed diagram of a horses foot, from the side and underneath.

Structure of the Horse's Foot

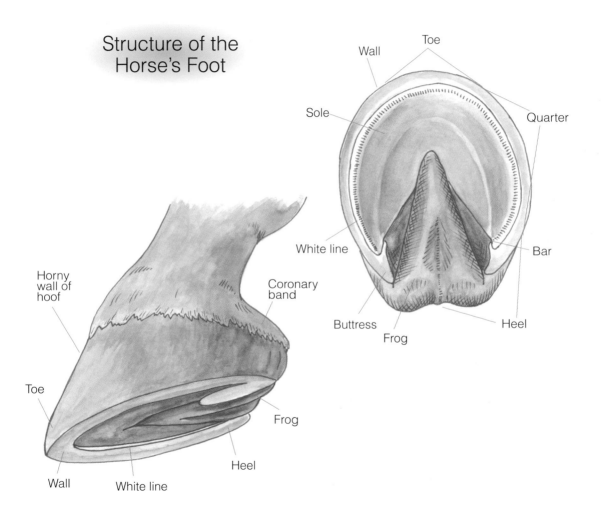

Wall

Toe

Sole

Quarter

White line

Bar

Horny wall of hoof

Coronary band

Buttress

Heel

Frog

Toe

Frog

Wall

White line

Heel

A large percentage of lamenesses stem from the foot, either following an injury such as a sharp object piercing the sole or due to poor foot shape or internal problems, which can be triggered by bad conformation. Corrective shoeing can sometimes help.

Bones

The main bone in the foot is the pedal bone. Above this, the short pastern extends from the lower leg down into the foot. The joint between the pedal bone and the short pastern is the coffin joint. Behind this is a small bone called the 'navicular' bone.

Other Structures

Inside the hoof wall are the laminae, which are like leaves of tissue attaching the wall to the pedal bone. The insensitive, horny laminae are on the outside, by the wall, with the sensitive laminae inside them.

Probably the largest non-bony structure in the foot is the digital or plantar cushion, a piece of tissue at the back of the foot below the bones. Below this and the pedal bone are the sensitive sole and frog, which line their equivalent insensitive external structures. At the top of the horse's foot is the coronet band. Inside, the coronet has an excellent blood supply to carry nutrients to the wall. There are also tendons and ligaments in the foot, which allow movement.

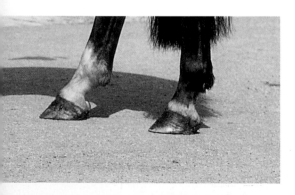

◄ A horse's feet are central to its wellbeing – lameness mostly originates in the foot.

► Here you can clearly see the wedge-shaped frog as distinct from the sole.

The Senses

The horse evolved as a grazing animal and its natural defence is flight not fight, so its senses are therefore highly developed to detect approaching danger.

Sight and Hearing

The horse's eyes are on the side of its head, giving it an excellent range of vision. With its head down grazing, the horse can see nearly all around it, although it does have limited vision directly in front and behind it. It is thought that horses may have a more limited colour vision than humans, or see colours differently. They see better in the dark, however, and can probably see further than humans.

Horses have finely tuned hearing. Their two large ears are highly mobile so that they can pick up sound from every direction. The brain analyses incoming sounds from both ears and works out from where the noises originate.

Taste, Smell and Touch

Anyone who has tried to feed a horse medicine knows that these animals have an acute sense of smell and taste. In the wild, these senses would prevent them from eating

◄ Curling the top lip back as seen is referred to as the flehmen response, or flehming, and facilitates horses to smell certain scents, particularly pheromones.

► Horses enjoy some touching. Nuzzling and chewing each other is an important part of socializing and bonding for horses, and also helps to remove parasites from hard to reach places.

poisonous plants, while smell would help them to recognize other members of their herd and to detect predators. Horses tasting or smelling something unusual will sometimes display the flehmen response, lifting the head and curling back the upper lip. Stallions also do this as part of sexual behaviour.

Horses are also sensitive to touch. They sometimes even have an involuntary reaction to it, such as twitching the skin to remove flies. They also enjoy some touching; horses will often groom each other with their teeth, and many horses relish the feel of being brushed by their rider.

Conformation

The horse's conformation describes its shape. Conformation is not just important to make a horse look attractive and move well for the show ring. A horse with good conformation is also likely to stay sound longer, be a more comfortable ride and be able to gallop faster and jump higher.

Although broadly speaking the same conformation traits are desirable whatever sort of horse you are examining, certain points are more important for different disciplines. For example, a horse with a ewe neck is never going to make a top dressage horse, but it may be a good jumper. And some horses do break the rules and defy average or poor conformation to stay sound and become excellent performers.

◄ A ewe neck has more muscling on the underside.

► When assessing conformation the horse must be examined on hard standing and in good light. It is also important to see the horse move on the straight, and in a circle on both reins.

Assessing Conformation

Assessing conformation is largely a matter of experience. It is more difficult to assess the conformation of a horse in poor condition (too fat, too thin or wrongly muscled) than that of one which is fit and well. Although some faults can be harder to recognize in the correctly muscled horse, an expert should still be able to pick out serious problems. Equally, an experienced person should be able to spot good conformation in a horse in poor condition.

When assessing a horse's conformation, start by taking an overall look at the animal. Are its different parts in proportion? Does it give an impression of kindness and good character? Next, move on to analyse its different parts.

Head and Neck

Look for a horse with a kind expression in its eye and an attractive head. Too much white showing in the eye can indicate bad temper, while small 'piggy' eyes can go with an obstinate nature.

If the horse's profile is concave, this is known as a 'dish face', and often signifies Arab or Welsh breeding. The opposite, a Roman nose, generally indicates heavy horse blood, but can be a sign of a genuine horse.

◄ A bull neck makes it hard for the horse to work correctly.

▶ High withers may cause problems with saddle fitting.

Make sure that the head is well set on the neck and that the horse is not 'thick through the gullet'. This will make it difficult for the animal to work in an outline.

The neck should be of good length for a comfortable ride and curve naturally out of the shoulder, with the crest well developed. A ewe neck (well-developed muscle underneath the neck and weak topline, a condition that can sometimes be improved with correct work), bull neck (short and thick) and swan neck (long neck which is dipped in front of the withers, then arched, with the highest point further back than the poll) will all make it hard for the horse to work correctly. If the neck is set too low on the shoulders, the horse will struggle to stay off the forehand and work 'uphill'.

Withers, Shoulder and Front Leg

The withers should be higher than the croup in the mature horse or the animal will find it very difficult to work 'uphill'. Young horses' hindquarters are often above the withers. Very high, prominent withers may cause problems with saddle fitting.

The horse should have a good angle from the wither to the point of shoulder. This angle dictates the length of its stride and should be the same as the angle of the pastern of the front legs. A horse with an upright shoulder will have a short stride and be less comfortable to ride.

The front legs should be a pair. Viewed from the front, the legs should not turn in or out. The forearms should be well muscled, and the cannon bones should be short because long cannon bones are likely to compromise the horse's soundness. The horse's 'bone' is assessed by measuring the circumference of its leg just below the knee and dictates how much weight it can carry. The amount of bone will vary depending on type, but a horse with too little bone will be weedy and weak.

The knees and fetlocks should be large, flat and well defined, not rounded. The elbow

▶ View of a horse leg that is 'back at the knee'.

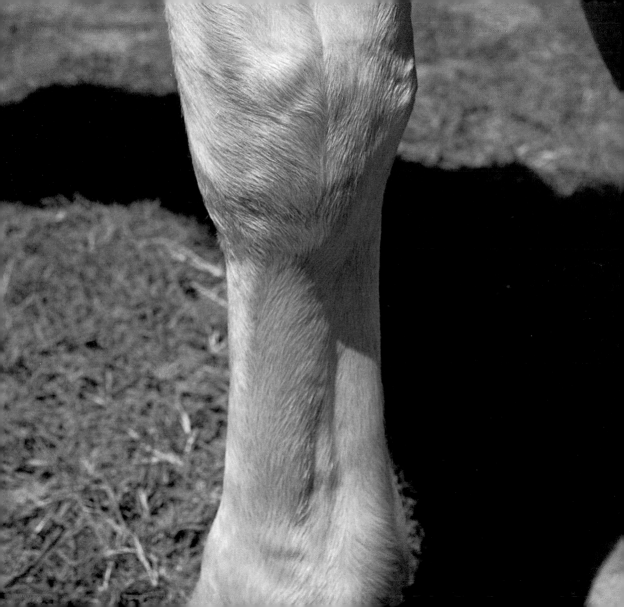

must not be 'tied in', as this will restrict movement. Seen from the side, if the knee appears to be behind the cannon bone, which comes out of it at a forward angle, the horse is 'back at the knee'; this is a serious fault that can lead to lameness. In contrast, being mildly 'over at the knee' is not usually a problem.

Chest, Body and Back

The chest should be broad enough (and the barrel deep enough through the girth) to give adequate room for the heart and lungs. If the chest is too narrow, with 'both front legs out of one hole', the horse is likely to brush (rub or knock its front legs against each other); if it is too wide, the action is likely to be rolling and uncomfortable. 'Well-sprung ribs' means that the ribs come well out from the backbone, giving a comfortable platform for the rider and room for the essential organs.

An excessively long back is likely to be weak, and such a horse will be harder to collect and keep together than one which is 'short-coupled'. A longer back is more common in mares, which need room to carry a foal. A dipped back is called a 'hollow', or 'sway', back and can develop with age, while a 'roach' back curves upwards towards and over the loins.

On a 'herring-gutted' horse, the underside of the body slopes steeply upwards towards the stifle. This is a conformation fault that can be seen whatever condition the horse is in, but many horses will 'run up light' and show this tendency to some extent after hard work.

◄ Hollow or sway backs, where the back dips behind the withers, can be seen in very elderly horses. The horse pictured is actually higher in his croup than withers, which exaggerates the condition.

► Poor hindleg conformation.

Hindquarters and Back Leg

The hindquarters should be wide, flat and well muscled. From behind, the hips should be level. A horse with a pronounced croup (buttocks) has a 'jumper's bump', while if the quarters slope sharply from croup to dock (top of the tail) the horse is 'goose-rumped'. Both can indicate a good jumper.

The horse should have good length from the point of hip to the point of buttock and be 'well let down' (good length from stifle to hock). From the side, the point of buttock and point of hock should form a straight line, which then follows down the back of the cannon bone to the fetlocks. If the hocks hang out behind it, the horse will find engagement difficult, and if the fetlocks are in front of the line the hocks will be too bent and weak. These are called 'sickle hocks'.

The hocks should be large and well defined. Viewed from behind, 'cow hocks' describe those which are turned in, with the toes turned out, while 'bowed hocks' are turned out, with the toes turned in. Both cause strain.

Feet

The front feet should be a pair in size, shape and slope, as should the back feet. The front feet will be more upright than the hind, and the slope should follow the

◄ The term 'flat feet' is used to describe a horse that lacks concavity in its soles. This is most common in the front feet, and is best seen by picking the feet up and looking at the underneath.

► Cow hocks can cause strain.

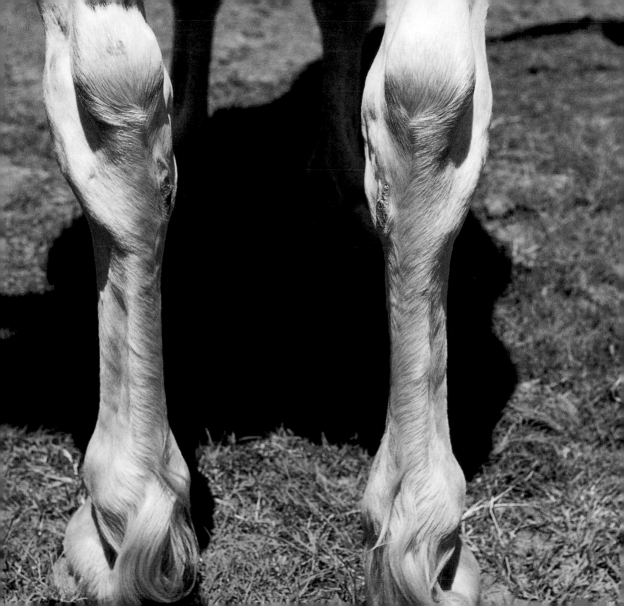

angle of the pastern for the best chance of soundness. Wide heels, a large frog (wedge-shaped pad on the bottom of the foot) and concave sole are desirable. Small, narrow or 'boxy' feet are likely to cause soundness problems. Flat feet, which are often large, too sloping and with low heels, are a trait seen particularly in Thoroughbreds, and due to the lack of concavity in the soles they are prone to bruising. Feet which turn either outwards or inwards (pigeon toes) can both put strain on the limbs.

Colours

Solid Colours

Probably the most common colour of horse is a bay. **Bay** horses are brown, with black points; the points being the mane, tail, muzzle, tips of the ears and lower legs. Bays can be 'bright', 'light' or 'dark'.

Horses can also be brown or **black** or **grey**. No horse is ever correctly described as white, even those that are pure white are known as grey. Dappled grey horses have ring-shaped markings of darker and lighter shades on their coats, while flea-bitten greys have specks of black or brown on their white coat. Iron greys are those with a steely, dark grey appearance.

▶ Bay – brown with black points – is most likely the most common colour of horse.

◀ All white horses are known as 'grey'.

Chestnut horses have a ginger or orange coat. Chestnuts come in 'light' or 'dark' shades, while 'liver' chestnuts have a deep liver colour. Some chestnuts have a pale mane and tail, known as 'flaxen'.

Dun horses are a yellowy brown colour, and vary in shade; a dun horse might be described as 'mouse', 'yellow', 'silver', 'blue' or 'golden'. Duns have black points, and also have a dorsal, or 'eel' stripe, which is a black line along the backbone. Some duns also have black stripes, known as zebra markings, on their legs.

Palomino horses have a yellowy gold coat, with a white mane and tail.

'Coloured' horses

Any horse of more than one colour, or which is an unusual colour, can be known as a coloured horse.

A piebald horse is black and white, while a **skewbald** is white and any other colour. **Roan** horses have white hairs and another colour interspersed through their coat. The most common roans are blue roans, where the hairs are white and black or brown, and strawberry roans, where the hairs are white and chestnut.

Spotted horses come in a number of common variations, including 'leopard', with dark spots on a white background; 'snowflake', which is the reverse; and 'blanket', a white rump with dark spots on it.

In the United States, some coloured horses and ponies are registered as pintos. **Pintos** can be a variety of breeds, but must meet specific colour requirements, while **Paint** horses are basically coloured horses with Quarter Horse or Thoroughbred blood. There are many terms and subdivisions, used mostly in the United States, for different coat patterns. In general, however, **tobianos** have a white coat, white legs and white across the back, with patches of colour.

Overos have a coloured coat, with splashes of white that rarely go across the back.

▶ Duns always have black points.

Changing Colour

Horses can change colour with age. Greys are usually born dark and become lighter as they get older. This process takes place at a different rate in different breeds and individuals.

Horses can also appear a different colour when sporting their thick winter coats to when they have their sleek summer coats. And if the horse is clipped to let it carry out its work more comfortably (more usual in winter, but sometimes carried out in summer, too), the clipped part of its coat may be quite a different shade.

Breed and Colour

Breed and colour are sometimes linked – for example, Fell ponies are most commonly black, dark brown or bay, although they can also be grey. Many breed societies will not accept coloured horses in their studbooks.

Colour and Superstition

There are many superstitions and prejudices about horse colours. Traditionally, chestnut mares have been seen as flighty and unreliable, although many owners of such horses will tell you this is not true. In some circles, coloured horses were seen as common or

◄ Blue roans have white hairs interspersed with black or brown.

► Skewbald colouring consists of patches of white coat with any other colour except black.

somehow undesirable for many years, but coloured horses are increasingly performing at the top level in many disciplines.

Markings

Many horses have some white on their head and legs. These markings are very useful for identification and will be drawn onto the horse's passport or other documentation, such as a vaccination certification.

Head

A blaze is a wide white mark, usually starting above the eyes and running between them down the front of the horse's face, with the white being broad enough to cover the nose bones. If the white covers the eyes, forehead and much of the muzzle, this is known as a 'white face'. A 'stripe' is a narrower white mark down the face. A 'star' is white on the forehead or between the eyes, and a 'snip' is white on the nose, perhaps extending into the nostrils. A horse can show these markings in combination, so it might have a star, then a gap in the middle of the face with no white markings before a snip. Or it may have a star which extends into a stripe.

Legs

A horse can have white markings on any, all or none of its legs. A stocking is when the white extends from the foot to between the fetlock and the knee or hock, while on a sock the white finishes at the fetlock or below. If a horse has patches of colour in the white, most commonly on the coronet band, these are called 'ermine marks'.

◀ A classic blaze mark on the head.

▶ An example of a star marking.

Acquired Markings

As well as markings the animal is born with, horses can have acquired markings. These can be the result of accidental damage. A horse may grow white hair after a cut, for example, and many horses have some white hairs on their withers where they have been rubbed by a saddle or rug.

Acquired markings also include those deliberately put on the horse for identification. Some horses are branded with a hot iron, resulting in a pattern in the coat, which identifies their breed or breeder. These brands are usually on the shoulder, hindquarters or saddle area. Freeze marking is a popular way of marking horses as a deterrent to thieves and to make the horse easier to identify if it is stolen. Horses are usually freeze-marked under the saddle. Superchilled markers are used, which destroy the pigment so the hair grows back white. Each horse is marked with a unique four-digit number. Grey and light coloured horses are given a bald freeze mark, so the markers are held on longer and the hair follicle is destroyed. This is usually done on the shoulder to prevent the saddle rubbing on a bald mark.

Other methods of identification include microchipping (where the horse has a tiny permanent unique chip inserted under the skin of its neck, which can be read with a special scanner) and stamping the horse's hooves with the owner's postcode (which has to be redone regularly, as it grows out).

Whorls

Whorls are like a human's hair parting; places where the hair swirls round to grow in a different direction. They are commonly found on the forehead, at the top of the neck and on the chest. Head and neck whorls, and those on other parts of the body on horses with few identifying features, are usually marked with a cross on the horse's passport or other identification document.

▶ In the United States, horses with white leg markings, such as these stockings, are described as 'chromey', meaning 'flashy'.

Behaviour and Psychology

Most horses today are kept for pleasure or competition. They are trained to carry humans and behave in a certain way. Although they live in an environment which is not natural for them, the majority of horses adapt and learn to fit into a society which is human- rather than equine-driven. Some of their natural responses may become muted, but horses do not lose their instincts, and many reactions that humans see as annoyances or faults are simply natural behaviour coming through.

Herd Instinct

In the wild, horses are herd animals, living in groups for company and protection. The herd leader is usually a mature female, with the group made up of females, foals and immature youngsters. As colts reach maturity, they will leave and form bachelor groups. A mature stallion will live

◄ This piebald is warning the palomino to keep its distance by flattening its ears and kicking out with its hind leg.

► Grooming, primarily along the neck, withers, back and flanks is an important part of bonding and socialization within the 'herd'.

on the edge of the herd, claiming his harem of mares by scent-marking piles of faeces and urination spots. The stallion's harem may incorporate a number of small bands, each under an alpha female, but his position is always vulnerable to challenge by a younger stallion.

Horses are therefore highly sociable animals, and many are unhappy if they have to live alone. They can also become distressed if they are left on their own in the short term. For example, if a horse is left in the field when its companions come in, it may gallop around or jump the fence to join them. Some horses are naturally leaders in the herd, while others are happy to follow. When a new group of horses are turned out together, there is likely to be some galloping around and squealing, as the horses sort out who is the boss.

Communication

Much of equine communication is through physical signals and body language. Some of these signals are easily recognizable by humans, such as laying back the ears as a sign of displeasure or aggression. Horses also use smell, releasing pheromones, which other horses can sense, from the skin glands, and touch, such as mutual grooming. Horses also communicate vocally, such as through squeals and whinnying.

Flight Instinct

Horses are naturally prey animals, herbivores that evolved to eat grass and run away from predators. Although horses will fight if forced to do so, their first instinct when confronted with danger is flight.

In the domesticated situation, this instinct means horses spook or shy away from unusual sights and sounds. Horses can often hear or see potential danger earlier than humans and will jump away quickly.

► Horses in the wild live in small groups (herds) that include several mares and youngsters, as seen, and are watched over normally. by just one stallion.

As horses are so big and strong, it is easy for humans to be hurt accidentally if they are not alert to this potential unpredictability.

Learning

Horses are creatures of habit and will be happiest if they have a routine in their daily lives and work. They are intelligent animals, with long memories of good or frightening experiences. They learn by repetition, and many are willing and even anxious to please. This means that they can be highly trained – for example, to take on narrow jumps on cross-country courses or perform difficult dressage movements.

Different Temperaments

Horses vary widely in their temperament. This is partly linked to their breed, so a Thoroughbred is likely to be more flighty and 'sharp' than a heavier type. But individuals are also different in their natures, and much is governed by the horse's treatment.

A horse's behaviour will be altered partly by its short-term management – for example, many horses are more relaxed if they spend longer in the field and less time cooped up in a stable. Much of the horse's later behaviour is dictated by how it is treated and trained during its first interaction with humans when it is a youngster.

◄ Being intelligent creatures, horses enjoy the challenge of training.

► This horse is being held while being groomed to prevent it from spooking or shying away. Both handlers should always be on the same side of the horse.

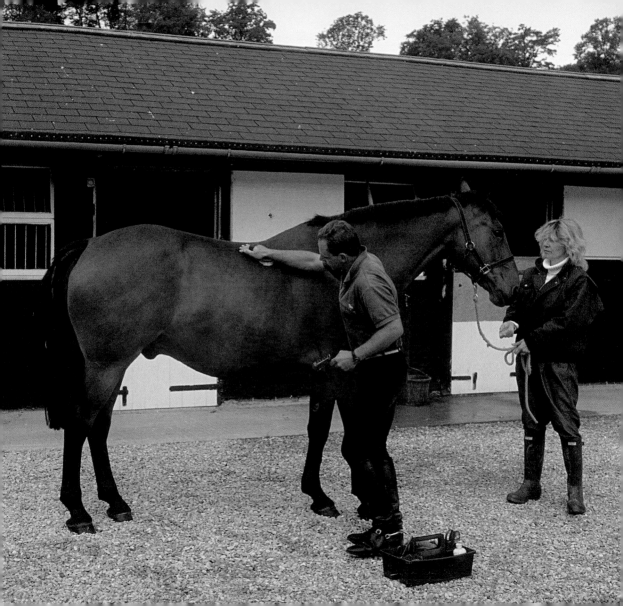

Getting Ready for your
Horse

Choosing and Buying a Horse

Choosing to become a horse owner is a major decision, one which should be carefully thought out, particularly if this is your first venture into owning horses. It is both exciting and easy to rush into buying the first horse you see. Take your time, and consult an expert. Make sure that you see a range of horses so that you develop an idea of what you want and, most importantly, what is suitable. Be prepared to keep looking until you find the right one.

It is worth taking the time to find the right horse when looking to buy. Once purchased the horse becomes a major part of your life with a strong bond forming between horse and owner.

Points to Consider

First, all prospective horse owners should ask themselves whether they should own a horse. Are you prepared to devote the necessary amount of time to looking after it? Do you have somewhere suitable to keep it? Perhaps most importantly, can you afford to buy one, and sustain the accompanying costs?

Horses are a big responsibility. They require care all year round, in all weathers, regardless of whether you are unwell or

► Choosing a horse is a big step. It is very important to understand the reasons for your choice and carry out as much research as possible.

busy. Do you have someone you can turn to for advice and support, and who could look after the horse in an emergency?

Are You Experienced Enough?

No one should buy a horse without having the knowledge and experience to look after it. Of course, you will learn a great deal as you go along, but a basic level of riding ability and a rudimentary understanding of a horse's needs are essential. Although it is lovely to have your horse at home, it is often more sensible to keep your first horse at a good livery yard. This should mean you will have help looking after it and can ask the yard owner for advice. Many people learn to ride in riding schools and, despite having reached quite a sophisticated standard of equitation, are surprised how different it is and how much hard work is involved in owning and caring for your own horse.

How Much Do You Want to Spend?

Horses can cost anything from a few hundred dollars or pounds to many millions. It is a good idea to work out your budget, then stick to it. Be realistic; you are not going to find your dream event horse for nothing, but be wary of spending tens of thousands on a first horse. You may decide horse owning is not for you, and it is best to stick a toe in the water before plunging in. Remember that the initial lump sum to purchase the horse is only the start. Make a careful list of what you will need to buy

◄ ► It can be beneficial to keep your horse at a good livery yard, where there are professionals on hand to help.

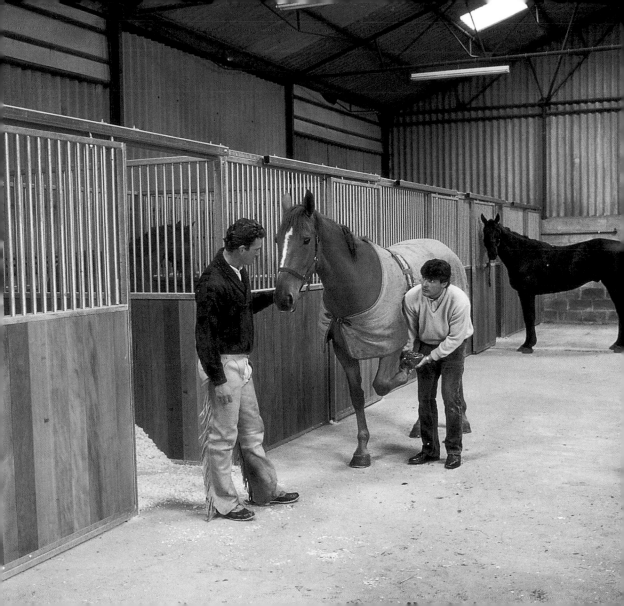

in the way of tack, rugs and grooming kit. Work out how much it will cost to keep it at livery or, if the horse is to live at home with you, what the extra costs will be in terms of electricity and water, as well as hay, hard feed, bedding, stable and fencing maintenance, grass upkeep and tools. Factor in vet's fees, as well as routine expenses such as vaccinations, worming and farriery.

What Sort of Horse?

There are so many different sorts of horses that it can be difficult to decide which one is suitable for you. Don't be too ambitious; it is often better to be under-horsed than over-horsed. Consult your instructor, who should have a good idea of what will suit. Consider in what circumstances you will be keeping it: if the horse is to live out in a field all the time, it may be better to get a hardy native breed than a thin-skinned Thoroughbred. What do you wish to do with it? If your ambitions lie in the show ring, you will need to choose very carefully a horse that is true to type with good conformation and good looks. If you are nervous, make sure you are looking for a sane, sensible horse; an ex-racehorse may be tempting and cheap, but would a sturdy half-bred or cob be more suitable?

Where to Look

There are many places to look for a horse to buy. The main ones are:

Trade Papers and Magazines

The equestrian press is often the best place to look for horses. Remember that all horses sound great in an advertisement; do not take all the seller says at face value. Local papers often have an equine section, and sometimes better value can be found here than in the classified sections of national magazines.

> ▶ Cob types such as this can be a wise choice, as they are often sensible in nature, quiet to handle and are good weight carriers.

The Internet

There has been a vast increase in the amount of horses advertised for sale on the Internet in recent years. A quick search will reveal many sites, with horses ranging from top competition animals to small ponies. Many horse dealers now have their own websites, which can be a useful tool, but check how often the ads are posted and updated. It is easy to fall in love with a horse that was sold months ago. Never buy a horse without going to see it, however, and check carefully that the horse you do see is indeed the one advertised.

Horse Dealers

The advantage of going to a dealer's yard is that often they will have a selection of horses to show you, rather than just one. As long as you check that the dealer has an excellent reputation within the horse world, this can be a good way to buy a first horse, as they are more likely than a private seller to take an unsuitable horse back. Their reputation relies on client satisfaction, and good dealers are experienced at finding the right horse for the right person.

Auctions

Some great bargains can be found at auction, but it is a big risk to take and best left to those with a good deal of experience.

◄ Care should be taken to cross reference sources on the internet.

► Sales such as this pictured should be treated with caution. If the inexperienced horse person is contemplating buying a horse from a sale, they should always take a professional horse person with them for advice.

What to Ask

Don't be afraid to ask the seller as many questions as you like, and do take a friend, ideally with lots of experience, with you.

- Before you arrive, ask for the horse to be left out in a field so that you can see it being caught and brought in.
- Look carefully at the horse and its conformation. Does it have any lumps, bumps or scars, and what is the explanation for them?
- Has it ever suffered from any serious veterinary problems?
- How old is the horse and how big is it? What sex is it?
- How is it bred?
- What has it done? Does it have a competition record? Has it been hunting?
- Why is it being sold?
- Does it bite, kick, buck, rear, or suffer from a stable vice such as crib-biting, wind-sucking or box-walking?
- Does the horse suffer from any seasonal problems, such as sweet itch in the summer or mud fever in the winter?

► When looking at a horse it should be seen trotting up on a hard surface in a straight line. Observe its movement from in front, from the side and from behind to check for soundness and to evaluate the way it travels.

- Is it vaccinated, and does it have a passport? (In the United Kingdom and Republic of Ireland, for instance, it is illegal to sell a horse without one.)
- Watch it being tacked up. How does it react to the bit being put in its mouth or the girth tightened? Does it stand still when it is being mounted?
- Ask to see it ridden, on the flat and over fences. In its home environment, expect it to go as well as it can.
- Ride it, first in an enclosed environment, then, if you like it, ask if you can take it for a short hack. This should give you a chance to see how it reacts to traffic.

Most importantly, ask yourself whether you like the horse, whether you feel confident around it, is it the sort you are looking for, and is it worth the money the seller is asking.

▲ Make sure you observe the horse being ridden.

▶ Don't forget to take a horse for a good trot and observe it's behaviour before you move forward with your purchase.

Environment

There are two main ways to keep a horse: principally outside (in a field) and principally inside (in a stable). Not all horses are suited to either. It is perfectly possible to keep a horse outside, rugged or unrugged, but it is useful to have a stable to bring it in to if necessary, such as for veterinary treatment. Hardy native types cope best with this sort of management. More highly bred horses may also cope, but many prefer to be stabled at night during the winter.

Grass-kept Horses

The bare minimum amount of land on which a horse can be kept is 0.4 ha (one acre), but it is much easier on a plot of 0.8–1.2 ha (two to three acres). This allows the land to be divided up and rested as necessary.

Fencing

Make sure that your field is well fenced. The best fencing is solid post-and-rails, with either a tall hedge or

◄ Horses must be provided with an adequately large shelter to protect them from the elements (hot and cold).

► Fresh water should be available at all times. Still water, such as in ponds, can become stagnant.

trees for shelter. But taut plain wire (*not* barbed wire) or a thick hedge can be used, although the latter must be checked regularly for gaps. The gate should be made of treated wood or metal, and be high enough to stop horses from jumping out. For your convenience, make sure that it is properly hung and has a secure fastening. If the gate opens on to a road, a chain and padlock are advisable. Check all fencing frequently for damage and weakness.

It is nice for horses to have a field shelter where they can escape the worst of the winter weather, and avoid the flies in the summer. If you are keeping more than one horse together, check that the shelter has a wide-enough entrance to prevent one horse trapping another in there, and some sort of bedding should be provided so that horses are not standing either in deep mud or on hard concrete. Always leave the cobwebs in the corners to catch the flies.

Water

Your field must have a clean, fresh supply of water. A tank linked to the water supply with a cock-and-ball system for replenishing it is ideal. A stream is fine, as long as it does not have a sandy bottom which the horse could suck up while drinking. If buckets are used, they will need to be filled up a couple of times a day, and more often in summer.

Not suitable are ponds without a stream running through them – the water becomes stagnant – or old baths with sharp edges. Remember that, in winter, water may freeze over and will need to have the ice broken up.

Grass

It can be tricky to provide your horse with enough grass, without it being too little or too much. Grass grows particularly lushly in the spring and autumn, and may need to be

▶ If your horse drinks from a tank, it is best to ensure that it is replenished regularly via a cock-and-ball system linked to the water supply.

restricted at these times. Small areas can be partitioned off with electric fencing. In the winter, the growth and quality may be insufficient and the horse's diet will need to be supplemented with good-quality hay.

Grass management is important. Investigate whether it needs fertilising, obviously removing all horses while this is done. Particularly long grass may need topping and the clippings removed. Buttercups are a sign that the grass is poor, and may need reseeding with a carefully selected assortment of grasses.

Check your field regularly for poisonous plants. These include ragwort, which has distinctive yellow flowers and, if eaten, is likely to prove lethal. Others include: yew; deadly nightshade; bracken; foxgloves; acorns; laburnum; privet; black and white bryony; ivy; locoweed; Johnson grass; field horsetail; tall fescue; perennial ryegrass; hemlock; common pokeweed; common cocklebur; hemp dogbane; white snakeroot; yellow and white sweetclover; common milkweed; and some mustards.

Management

All horses kept at grass need checking twice a day. They should be groomed less than stable-kept horses in order to preserve the coat's natural oils, which help to keep the horse warm and waterproof. Rugs should be removed and replaced every day, and feet checked for stones.

◄ Some horses (in particular native pony breeds) are able to winter out without being rugged, but others will need a waterproof and weatherproof rug such as seen in this picture.

► This is not an ideal way to feed hay as much is wasted, and there is a chance of bullying. It is better to leave a number of small piles of hay that allows each horse its own.

If you are feeding several horses in the field, space out the feeds or piles of hay to avoid fights, and to ensure each horse gets enough.

Stable-kept Horses

The Stable

A pony stable should be a minimum of 3.6 m x 3 m (12 ft x 10 ft); a horse should not be kept in a stable less than 3.6 m x 3.6 m (12 ft x 12 ft), ideally made of stone, which has the advantage of being cool in the summer and warm in the winter. But there are many modern stable companies who will build you durable, well-designed wooden stables at a reasonable cost.

It is useful to have hard standing outside the stable so that you can tie your horse up outside to be groomed and to be mucked out. Inside, the floor should slope slightly towards a drain at the front of the stable, so that urine does not collect. The stable door should be at least 1.1 m (3 ft 7 in) high, and fastened by bolts at both the top and the bottom.

The stable must be well ventilated. It is better for horses to be well rugged in cold weather than for the stable to get stuffy. Also, all light switches and fittings should be covered and out of the reach of the horse.

◄ Wood chips and shavings are a good form of bedding. They are very absorbent and easy to work with. They should be stored somewhere dry, for example a barn such as that pictured.

Bedding

There are many types of bedding, and you should consider which suits you and your horse best. Do not be tempted to skimp on bedding; horses like to lie down and should be able to do so in comfort and without damaging their knees and hocks.

Straw is warm, can be banked high at the sides and drains well. It is also the cheapest form of bedding, coming either in small bales or big round ones. But some horses suffer from dust allergies, which can cause respiratory problems. These animals will need a dust-free form of bedding, such as good-quality shavings, woodchip or paper. Hemp is a new, dust-free form of bedding, but can be quite expensive.

Shavings are easy to muck out and warm, but can get very wet and heavy because they do not drain well.

Well-fitted rubber matting on top of the stable floor stops horses having to stand on cold concrete and provides support for their feet and joints. Mats must be taken up and scrubbed from time to time.

Mucking out

You can either muck your horse out completely every day, removing all droppings and wet patches, or 'deep-litter' the bed. This means picking up the droppings, then putting more bedding on top to absorb the wet. A thick,

◀ If using an automatic drinking system the bowl should be regularly cleaned out. It is preferable to use a system with inbuilt gauges to measure the amount each horse is drinking.

▶ Mucking out is best done when the horse is not in the stable so a more thorough job can be carried out.

warm bed can be built up like this, but it will need totally removing about once a month, and it is more difficult to keep horses and rugs clean with this system. Muck heaps should be placed away from the stable, away from any water supply and downwind of the yard to prevent dirty straw being blown back.

Water

Water can be provided either in buckets, which need filling up and cleaning out, or by way of an automatic drinker which self-fills as the horse drinks. This is obviously less labour-intensive, but some horses do not like to drink from these, and it is impossible to check how much a horse is drinking daily.

Hay and Feed

Hay should be fed in a net, which must be tied up high enough to prevent a horse from getting its hoof caught in it, but slightly lower than eye level so that seeds do not fall into the horse's eyes; on a rack; or in piles on the floor. This last method is more wasteful, but is also more natural as the horse feeds with its head down, as it does in the wild. Feed can be placed in a manger, which will need regular cleaning out; in buckets, which may be in danger of being kicked over; or in a trough which can be clipped straight on to a horse's door.

Tack and Feed Rooms

Tack rooms must be properly secured, with substantial locks and an alarm system. All tack should be marked, as should rugs.

Feed rooms should also be kept locked. Feed bags should be placed in bins or at least on pallets to prevent the bags from becoming soggy. A tap with hot running water will make life easier.

▶ The tack room, everything in order, clean and well marked.

Exercise

Horses cannot just be left in their stables all day. If they are not turned out for a few hours, which is the best and most natural way of managing them, they must be properly exercised, either ridden or on the lunge, every day.

Rugs

If a horse is kept in a stable during the winter, it can actually become colder than its grass-kept counterpart because it is not moving around and keeping warm. It will therefore need rugging, particularly if it has been clipped. Modern stable rugs, made of nylon with padded fillings, come in several weights from light to heavy. It is good practice to use a thin cotton sheet as the bottom layer, which should be washed once a week. This saves the rest of your rugs from getting dirty and keeps the horse cleaner. All rugs should be washed and, if they are outdoor rugs, re-waterproofed, a couple of times a year.

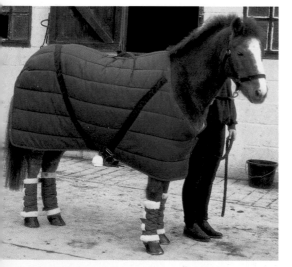

Outdoor rugs are called 'New Zealand rugs', and are both warm and waterproof. If a horse comes in from the field wet, it may be better to leave the rug to dry on the horse if you do not have a system of drying the rug quickly, as it is unpleasant for a horse to have a cold, damp rug put back on in the morning.

▶ Stable-kept horses must be turned out for a period of time daily, or exercised. They cannot be kept in for days at a time, it is detrimental to their physical and mental health – the exception being in the case of illness or injury.

Travelling with a Horse

Everything possible should be done to ensure that a horse has a good travelling experience. Bad travellers have been made that way, usually by bad driving, and it may well be difficult to re-establish their confidence.

Clothing

Horses should be travelled with adequate leg protection, be it travelling boots or bandages. The former are much easier to put on, particularly for inexperienced owners, but bandages may be more suitable on very long journeys because, if applied correctly, they provide a degree of leg support.

A tail bandage and tail guard will keep the tail from being rubbed and protect it. Do not, however, put the tail bandage on excessively tightly. A poll guard, made from foam or a bandage wrapped around the headpiece, is advisable on long journeys and for bad travellers.

Rugs will depend on the weather. In the summer, a sweatsheet or cotton sheet may be enough; in winter, a sweatsheet and thick wool travelling rug with a surcingle (a type of girth or band used to keep a blanket, saddle or pack secure round the middle) to keep them in place might be needed.

◄ Always make sure your horse is clothed appropriately for the weather on the journey and that its legs are protected.

► It is preferable to load horses and ponies using two handlers, as seen. Always keep the horse or pony nice and straight when walking up the ramp to encourage it to load properly.

Transport

Horses travel either in a special lorry (truck) or a horse trailer pulled by a four-wheel drive vehicle. Each should have rubber matting and a small amount of bedding on the floor, and must be well maintained and frequently checked for safety.

Horses often like to spread their legs for balance when travelling, and for this reason it is safer to have partitions that are not solidly attached to the floor. Always drive slowly and carefully, and remember that you will have to anticipate braking and turning much sooner than you would in a car.

Journeys

Plan long journeys carefully, and arrange to have stops every three hours. This rests horses and is an opportunity to give them a drink and replenish their haynets. You might also walk them around to stretch their legs, but never unbox on the side of the road, and make sure you will be able to get them to load again, otherwise it might be safer to leave them in the box until you get to your destination.

▶ Ensure the travelling horse's haynet is kept stocked, and stop regularly on long journeys to give them a drink. Travelling with a horse takes planning.

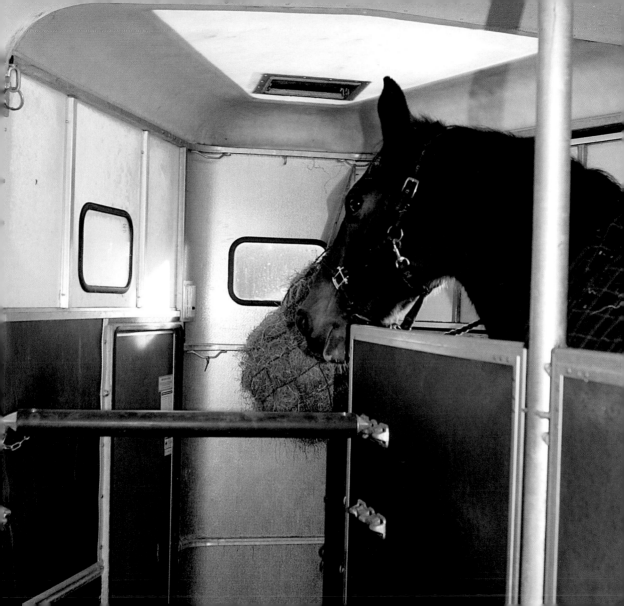

Tack and Equipment

It is easy to accumulate large amounts of tack and equipment, such as boots and rugs, for your horse, most of which you will use only once and which can cost you an absolute bomb. Invest in smaller amounts of the best-quality saddlery you can afford, and clean and maintain it carefully to ensure that it lasts. Also, make sure that it is not left lying around where it could easily be stolen: there is a considerable market in second-hand tack of doubtful provenance. See also pages 128–34 and 182 for information on Grooming Kit and Riding Gear respectively.

Saddles, Girths and Stirrups

Saddles

A good saddle is essential, and should be treated as an investment. It should be comfortable for both horse and rider, and expert advice from a saddle fitter should be sought. The three most popular types of saddle are:

- **General-purpose saddle** This is designed for all types of riding and general activities. It is sensible to buy this as a first saddle, as it can be used for both dressage and jumping. It will be fairly forward-cut without being as extreme as a jumping saddle, with a knee roll.

▶ The deep seat of the dressage saddle helps to stabilize the rider's position, while the long and straight flaps encourage the leg to lie in the correct position.

- **Jumping saddle** This usually has a flatter seat than a dressage saddle, and is designed for riding with short stirrups, so has a forward-cut saddle flap and knee and thigh rolls to help keep the rider's leg in place.

- **Dressage saddle** This is generally the most deep-seated saddle and often has a high cantle. The stirrup bars are further back than on a saddle predominantly used for jumping. The girth straps are longer than usual, and it is used with a short girth, to prevent the girth buckle lying under the rider's thigh.

Girths

Girths secure the saddle on a horse's back, and it is really important that they fit well and are in good repair. Check the stitching regularly. Girth sizes are determined by how long they are from end to end, including the buckle, and are usually measured in inches.

There are three main types of leather girth: the three-fold, where a single piece of leather is cut straight and folded over to form three layers; the Balding, which starts straight, with two buckles, but divides into three strips which cross over and are stitched together to reduce the width of the girth behind the horse's elbow where it could rub; and the Atherstone, which is also shaped to provide comfort for the horse, but is one solid strip of leather.

Girths can also be made of webbing, soft nylon or synthetic fabrics, which are easy to wash, but do not last as long as leather girths, string and a variety of synthetic leathers.

Stirrups

Stirrup leathers and stirrup irons should be of good quality and well maintained; it is not much fun if your stirrup leather breaks halfway around a cross-country course or

▶ From left to right the girths are: an Atherstone, a dressage girth, an Atherstone and a string or nylon girth – these are rarely used now in English riding, but are still relatively popular for use on Western saddles.

during a long-distance ride. Irons should be made of stainless steel, not nickel, which has a tendency to wear thin and break. They should be large enough to allow about 1 cm (½ in) at each side of the rider's foot; getting your foot stuck in the iron is very dangerous if you fall off. But don't use stirrup irons which are too big and allow the whole foot to slip through. Rubber treads fitted to the irons are a good idea, as they prevent the foot from slipping.

Stirrup leathers are made of ordinary leather (cowhide), rawhide or buffalo hide. The leathers tend to stretch when new, so check that the holes are still level with one another. It is also a good idea to switch the leathers over from time to time, as the one on the left stretches more because of the additional pressure of the rider mounting and dismounting.

▲ The solid stainless steel stirrup is the traditional type, while the stirrup with the black sides is a revolutionary new safety stirrup designed by Sprenger.

▲ These are safety stirrups, which are particularly popular for children. In the event of a fall, the elastic side pops open, which prevents the foot becoming stuck.

Bridles and Bits

There are three main types of bridle: snaffles (any bridle used with one bit), double bridles (with two bits) and bitless bridles.

The Snaffle Bridle

The snaffle bridle (see image on previous page) is made up of the following parts:

- **Headpiece and throatlash** Made from the same piece of leather, the headpiece goes over the top of the horse's head and, in conjunction with the cheekpieces, keeps the bit in the horse's mouth. The throatlash extends down from the headpiece, and fastens around the horse's throat to secure the bridle.
- **Browband** This attaches to the headpiece and goes around the brow at the front of the horse's head to prevent the headpiece slipping back.
- **Cheekpieces** These keep the bit in place by attaching to the headpiece and the bit rings.
- **Bit** This is the main device for communicating with the horse, and comes in an almost infinite variety of shapes, sizes and materials. The cheekpieces and reins are attached to the bit by buckles, hooked billets or stitching.
- **Reins** These are the long strips of leather between the bit and the rider's hands, down which communication signals are passed. Make sure that they are the correct width for the rider's hands, and the right length.
- **Noseband** This aid to control fits around the horse's nose and is a separate piece of leather which attaches only to itself, but fits through the browband loops and over the head under the headpiece. It comes in a variety of forms, such as the cavesson, which is the standard simple noseband; the drop, which fits below the bit and is stronger; and the 'flash', which is a combination of the two.

> ▶ Double bridles should only be used on horses that have reached a certain level in their training, and are most commonly used for upper levels of dressage, or for showing.

The Double Bridle

This has two bits, called the 'bridoon' (snaffle) and the 'curb', and an extra headpiece and cheekpiece, called a 'slip-head' is used to secure the bridoon. They are buckled on the right side, whereas all other bridle straps are fastened on the left. The curb bit must have a curb chain attached to it, and a lip strap should be threaded through the 'fly' (extra) link in the centre of the curb chain to hold it in place. As there are two bits, there are also two sets of reins, and it is a good idea to make these slightly different to each other so that it is easy to tell which set controls which bit.

The Bitless Bridle

These are usually used to keep a horse with a sore mouth in work while the damage heals, but can be useful if a horse is particularly fussy or difficult in his mouth. They rely on nose pressure and leverage to control the horse. The most common form is the hackamore.

Bits

The snaffle is the basic schooling bit and the most commonly used bit. It comes in a range of forms with different mouthpieces and rings or cheeks, each of which have a different action in the horse's mouth. Some popular ones include the eggbutt snaffle, the loose-ring snaffle, the French link, the straight-bar snaffle, the Dr Bristol or the hanging-cheek snaffle. Gags are a type of snaffle, but more severe than most and, as well as acting on various parts of the horse's mouth, also apply poll pressure.

Pelhams are a combination of the curb and the bridoon from a double bridle in one bit. Critics say that this blunts the effectiveness of the bits and is a less sensitive aid, but many horses go well in them. They should be

▶ Gags should be used with two reins, as seen here. They are a severe bit and exert pressure on the poll, while also applying upward pressure to the corner of the mouth that acts to raise the head.

worn with a curb chain. Some riders have 'roundings', which enable just one rein to be used. Some pelhams, such as the Kimblewick, are designed to be used with a single rein, but most, such as the Rugby, globe, half-moon or broken, are used with two reins.

Martingales and Reins

There are three types of martingale: standing, running and Irish.

Standing Martingale

This is used to stop the horse raising its head too high. It consists of a piece of leather, which loops around the girth and passes between the horse's front legs, through a supporting loop on the neck strap, to the cavesson noseband. It should not be fitted too tightly and should not be used to hold the horse's head down.

Running Martingale

This is a more moderate way of encouraging the horse not to carry its head too high, and takes effect only when the horse raises its head beyond the angle of control. It attaches to the girth between the forelegs; after it

◄ Standing martingales attach to the back of a cavesson noseband, and prevent the horse from raising its head above a certain level.

► Running martingales should always be used in conjunction with rubber martingale stops. These are positioned on the rein between the bit ring and the martingale ring.

passes through the rubber ring on the neck strap that holds it in place, it divides into two. Each of these two ends is fitted with a metal ring, through which the reins are passed. Make sure that it is not too tight or, more commonly, too loose. As a rough guide, when the martingale is attached to the girth and both rings are taken to one side, it should be long enough to reach the horse's withers.

Irish Martingale

This is simply two metal rings connected by a leather strap approximately 10 cm (4 in) long. The reins are threaded through it under the horse's neck. It is most commonly seen in racing, and is used to keep the horse's reins in place and stop them flying over its head.

Reins

Reins are available in several materials:

- **Leather** Plain leather is very smart, gives the best feel and is most correct in the show ring, but can become slippery in the rain or on a sweaty horse. Plaited leather is less slippery, but is expensive and can be difficult to clean.
- **Rubber** Rubber-covered leather, on one side of the rein or both, gives the best grip. When these reins become tatty, they can often be re-covered with rubber by a saddler, as long as the leather underneath is sound.

◄ Reins come in different materials. Here rubber reins are shown, as well as webbing reins with leather stops on the right.

► Irish martingales are especially useful in the case of a fall.

- **Webbing** These give good grip and, if they have leather 'bars' on them, do not slip.
- **String** These are often suitable for children because they are particularly pliable and should not slip, but may not be smart enough for competing adults.

Lungeing reins Lungeing reins are long webbing reins that fix on to a lungeing cavesson (a special type of padded leather headcollar used for lungeing) and allow the horse to move in a large circle around the lunger. They should be at least 7 m (23 ft) long and have a rotating clip joint.

Side reins Side reins are used when lungeing a horse, and run from the bit to the saddle or surcingle to encourage correct carriage and flexion. They are made from webbing or leather, sometimes with added elastic inserts for flexibility. They should be carefully fitted and adjusted by an experienced person, and must be the same length each side. It is advisable to warm the horse up on the lunge without them, then clip on the side reins when the horse is ready to work.

Lead reins Lead reins, made out of webbing and leather, attach via two clips to each bit ring. They are used for leading animals in hand, such as stallions, and in in-hand and leading-rein classes in the show ring.

Boots

There are many types of boots designed to stop the horse from injuring itself or being injured. The main ones are travelling boots, brushing boots, over-reach boots, knee boots and hock boots.

Travelling Boots

These boots are made of synthetic fibre, either padded or lined with fleece, and fastened with Velcro. They cover the whole lower leg from

► There are several kinds of rein available. These are leather.

just above or just below the knee or hock to the coronet band. They must fit correctly and not slip down. It is hardly ever necessary to travel horses in bandages now, except on particularly long journeys.

Knee Boots and Hock Boots

These also protect the horse while travelling and are made of thick felt or synthetic material. They are sometimes worn for exercising on the road and for hunting in country where there are walls to be jumped. The top straps must be done up tightly and the bottom loosely, so that there is no restriction of leg movement.

Brushing Boots

These are worn while the horse is being ridden, and protect the cannon bones and the sensitive structures in that area, such as tendons and ligaments, from damage. They are shaped to fit the contours of the leg, and come in different sizes. The fastenings should be on the outside of the leg with the strap ends pointing backwards. They are made of leather, Neoprene and synthetic fibres.

Over-reach Boots

These fit around the lower pastern and hoof, protecting the coronet band and bulb of the heel. Simple over-reach boots are made of a single piece of ridged rubber and are pulled on; more sophisticated designs are made from padded synthetic materials, are shaped and do up with straps.

◄ Over-reach boots protect the heel and coronet band.

► Travelling boots are typically made from heavy duty cotton or synthetic materials.

Rugs

Not all horses need to wear rugs, but horses which have been clipped or those with fine coats will need extra protection from the cold and bad weather.

Turnout Rugs

Called 'New Zealand rugs', these are designed for outdoor use. They should be both warm and waterproof. Old-fashioned canvas lined with wool is satisfactory but heavy, and there are many modern rugs which are light, easy to handle, hardwearing, warm and weather-resistant. They are fastened with cross-surcingles under the horse's stomach, and often have leg straps or fillet strings under the tail. It is important that they fit well, allow for movement and do not rub.

Stable Rugs

A variety of rugs for indoor use is available. They come in all fabrics, and are padded to different weights. The less bulky ones are machine-washable, and it is a good

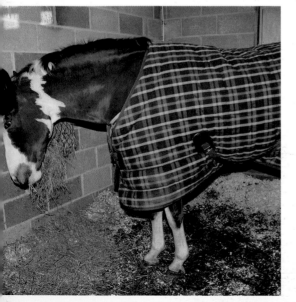

◄ Most modern rugs fasten using cross straps beneath the belly, as seen, which have largely replaced surcingles. Cross straps are more comfortable for the horse, but must be done up tightly enough to prevent a foot becoming caught.

▶ Some sweat rugs, such as this one, are called 'coolers'. The fabric works to actively wick moisture away from the horse, and help to dry the hot or wet horse more efficiently, cutting down on the chance of chilling.

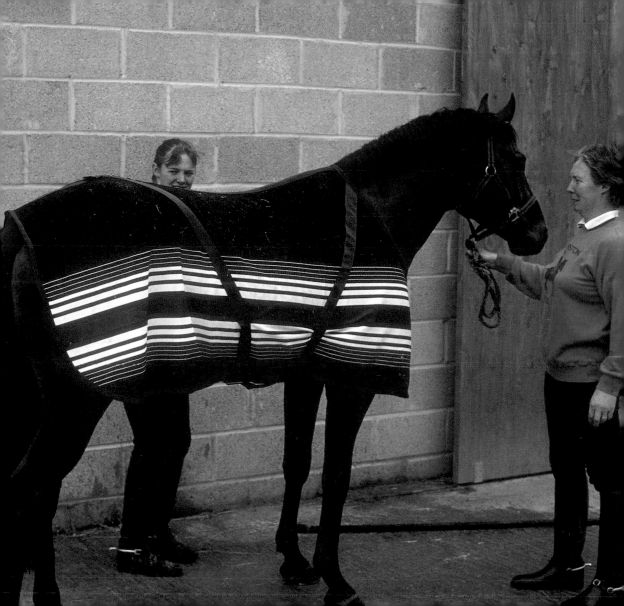

idea to use a cotton sheet underneath the stable rug to help keep both the rug and the horse clean. In really cold conditions, a cheap duvet or comforter can be used between layers of rugs and held in place with a surcingle.

Sweat Rugs

These are made of cotton mesh, synthetic 'breathable' fabrics or towelling, and are used on a sweating horse while it cools down to prevent chills, while travelling or to help dry a horse after it has been bathed.

Summer Sheets

These are made of cotton and are used as an under-rug, for travelling in summer, or to protect the clean, groomed horse from dust and flies.

Equipment Care

Tack

Saddles, stirrups, bridles and martingales should all be cleaned regularly. Using a cloth and warm water, remove all the mud, grease and scurf from tack, then rub in glycerine saddle soap with a sponge. The bottoms of saddles and bits should be washed after each ride, and numnahs (saddle pads) and saddle cloths should be washed as soon as they become dirty: this may be after each ride, and certainly if the horse has sweated much. From time to time, take the bridle to pieces and clean each part separately before putting it back together. Girths should be washed to remove sweat and mud and to prevent girth galls.

> ▶ All tack should be cleaned regularly. Glycerine saddle soap can be rubbed in after removing mud and dirt.

Give your tack a good inspection every six months, and check for signs or wear and tear. Never compromise on safety, and take anything with loose stitching to the menders. Check your saddle tree by holding the pommel and cantle, and squeezing together gently. If the leather on the seat wrinkles, it may have a broken tree. Check that bits have not developed sharp edges or are not wearing thin.

Rugs

Stable rugs and sweat rugs, if made from modern synthetic materials, can be washed and dried. Older, heavier rugs, such as those made from jute, will not wash easily, and these should be combined with a washable sheet as an under-rug, they can also be brushed. Some outdoor rugs can be washed,

but they will need re-waterproofing afterwards. Generally, scrubbing the worst of the mud and stains off is enough, although there are specialist rug washers who will wash and mend your rugs for you. Check all bindings and straps regularly; horses are good at breaking them.

Boots and Bandages

These should be washed, either in a machine or, if leather, by hand and soaped, after each wearing. Fastenings should be repaired and replaced as necessary.

> ▶ Store tack neatly and carefully using proper saddle racks and
> bridle pegs, and in a dry, clean area. This will help to keep it in
> good working order. The saddle in particular needs to rest on a
> proper stand to help keep the tree and flocking even and free
> from damage.

Caring for & Riding Your

Horse

Feeding

When you have bought your horse, check what its previous owner has been feeding it. This is important not only as a guide, but also because abrupt changes in a horse's diet are not advisable. You will also need to know about the principal rules of feeding, how much you should feed your horse and the different types of feed available. It is also important that you understand how different feeds break down into the three main types and ensure that you feed your horse in the correct combination and proportions.

Principal Rules of Feeding

- Feed small amounts of food regularly.
- Feed the best-quality food that you can afford. Cheap food is a waste of money, as its nutritional values are low.
- Feed according to the type of horse, its temperament, the amount of work it is doing and the condition it is in.
- Make sure that clean, fresh water is always available.
- Introduce changes to a feeding routine gradually, so that the bacteria in the horse's intestine have time to adapt accordingly.
- Feed something succulent every day.

◄ Buy the best you can afford – buying in bulk will save money, if you have the room to store it.

- Horses are creatures of habit and thrive on routine. Feed at approximately the same time every day.
- Don't feed immediately before or after exercise.
- Make sure that all feed and water buckets are cleaned regularly.

▲ Most of a horse's diet should be grass or hay.

▶ Horses are 'trickle feeders', that is their digestive
system is designed to cope with small amounts of
food fairly continuously. Horses in the wild will
graze for up to 18 hours a day.

How Much Should You Feed Your Horse?

It is not easy to work out how much your new horse needs feeding, and it can be a case of trial and error. The following calculation should provide a rough guide that you can adapt to your own horse:

Take the horse's weight in kilograms (either weigh it on a weighbridge or use a weight tape), and multiply it by 2.5. Divide the total by 100. The resulting figure is how much total food the horse requires per day. So a 16-hh horse might weigh 600 kg (600 x 2.5 / 100 = 15). This means that the horse should receive 15 kg of food.

Horses are grazing animals, and most of their diet should be grass or hay. For a horse in medium work, a good rule of thumb is that 70 per cent of its diet should be roughage, and 30 per cent should be made up of concentrates, such as oats, barley, sugar beet, etc.

This is obviously dependent on the horse's age, temperament and size. A Welsh pony will very rarely need concentrates in its diet and will survive well on

relatively poor grazing, while a fit Thoroughbred may need quite large amounts of concentrates to supply the energy it needs.

Feed Types

Feed is split into three main groups: roughage, concentrates, and vitamins and minerals.

Roughage

For most horses and ponies, roughage means **grass**, which should almost always provide the main part of a horse's diet. Mature horses in little or no work are unlikely to need anything else, as is the case with small native ponies. **Hay** is dried baled grass, and is fed in the winter when grass is poor and lacking.

Other forms of fibre include **haylage**, which is richer than hay and may not be suitable for native ponies and horses who suffer from obesity. **Chaff** is chopped hay or straw, and can be fed to bulk out small feeds and to prevent a horse bolting its food too quickly.

Concentrates

These are divided into **mixes and nuts**, and '**straights**'. 'Straights' are oats, barley, sugar beet and linseed. Mixes and nuts are these core components mixed together in varying quantities to form a range of pre-balanced feeds for all types of horses.

Barley should be cooked for at least two hours before feeding or bought in a pre-cooked formula, as it

▶ From top clockwise: rolled oats, horse and pony nuts (also called cubes or pellets), and flaked barley.

swells in a horse's stomach. It is a carbohydrate-rich food that is good at putting on condition and giving slow-releasing energy.

Oats should be fed crushed, rolled or cooked. They are easily digestible and palatable, but are high in energy and unsuitable for many types of horses and ponies.

Sugar beet is a by-product of the sugar industry, and therefore high in energy and very palatable. It is useful for putting on weight and for tempting shy feeders to eat. It comes in cubes, which must be soaked in cold water for 24 hours before feeding, or shreds, which should be soaked for 12 hours.

Linseed is poisonous to horses unless is it is cooked until the shiny seeds split and become jelly-like. Fed in small quantities, it is excellent for putting on condition.

Vitamins and Minerals

Many horse owners like to give their animals extra vitamins and minerals, often unnecessarily. Sometimes there is a need to supplement the horse's usual diet, but it is wise to consult an expert first. A salt or mineral lick is often popular. Other supplements such as garlic, for respiration, and various additives to improve hoof quality or aid joint suppleness can be useful. But it is easy to spend a fortune on fashionable products that your horse really does not need.

▶ The small bowl of pellets shows sugar beet before it has been soaked. Underneath is a large bowl of soaked sugar beet that is now ready for feeding.

Grooming and Maintaining

Regular grooming should be part of your daily routine with your horse. It keeps your horse's skin and coat healthy and clean. Horses that are stable-kept should be groomed more thoroughly than those that are kept on grass, as they have less need of the coat's natural oils and have a tendency to become scurfy underneath their rugs. It is also an opportunity to spend time with your horse and to bond with it outside of a ridden situation.

Grooming Kit

The term 'grooming kit' is given to the collection of brushes and tools that we use to clean our horses. Here are some of the most useful:

◄ The dandy brush has stiff bristles and is useful for removing mud and dirt from the legs in particular. Avoid using on sensitive areas such as the head, or on the mane or tail.

► From left to right starting at the bottom, a plastic curry comb (red), a dandy brush, a water brush, a rubber curry comb (black), a tail comb, a metal curry comb, a hoof pick, a body brush (dark bristles in middle, pale bristles round edge), a small comb and a sponge. The folded material is a stable rubber.

Dandy Brush

This stiff brush is used to remove mud, and is used on the legs and body. Avoid using on sensitive clipped areas or on the mane or tail.

Body Brush

A body brush is a soft-bristled brush used to deep-clean scurf from the coat. It is used on the whole body, in conjunction with a metal curry comb. Also use to brush out the tail and on delicate areas such as the head.

Curry Comb

A plastic or rubber-toothed curry comb can be used in small circular motions on the coat to loosen and remove mud, excess hair (when the horse is shedding its coat) and scurf. It can be useful on sensitive horses that object to hard brushing with a dandy brush. Metal curry combs should be used only to clean dirt and scurf out of a body brush, and not on the horse itself.

Hoof Pick

This is a blunt metal or tough plastic hook which is used to remove dirt and stones from horses' hooves. Take care with the sensitive parts of the hoof, and always pick downwards away from the heel to avoid damaging the frog.

Mane Comb

A wide-toothed comb of metal or plastic is used to comb out the mane, and can be used gently on the tail.

> ► The body brush is a soft bristled brush used for removing dirt, dust and dead hair from the coat. It should be used in conjunction with a metal curry comb, which is used to clean the brush, never on the horse.

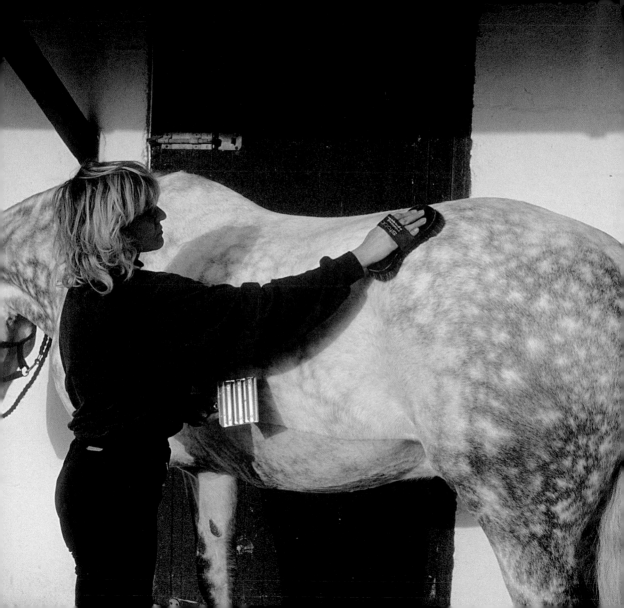

Water Brush

A soft brush with close-set bristles, this brush is used with water to remove stains from the horse's coat and sweat marks. It can be used for cleaning hooves and for laying manes and tails tidily.

Sponge

Sponges are used for washing horses or for cleaning areas such as the eyes, nose and dock.

Shampoo

Horses who live outside most of the time shouldn't be washed often because of the loss of the coat's natural oils. When you do wash your horse, such as after strenuous exercise or before a competition, use special horse shampoos which are gentler than the ones we use. Some horses love a bath on a hot day to cool down; if you must bathe them on cold days, use warm water and dry them thoroughly.

Sweat Scraper

This is a tool with a handle and a curved rubber strip with which you scrape off excess water after washing your horse down.

Hoof Oil

Hoof oil, applied with a small brush, is a bit like nail polish for horses and is a cosmetic touch used to make them look smart on competition and hunting days. It has a drying effect on the hoof, and should be used on special occasions such as high days and holidays.

▶ Hoof oil really enhances the look of the feet and should be used when showing and competing.

Stable Rubber

This is a finishing cloth used to provide gloss to a coat and remove final traces of scurf. It is often used in the show ring to make the horse look its best just before the judge examines it.

Scissors

Round-ended, blunt scissors can be used to trim unwanted hair around the horse's chin and muzzle, and remove feather from their fetlock joints. They are also used to shorten the tail, but never on the mane.

Grooming Tips

How to Wash a Tail

Soak the tail in a bucket of lukewarm water to loosen the dirt. If you cannot fit the whole tail in a bucket, wet the top part of the dock with a water brush. Shampoo with a special equine shampoo, and rub vigorously. Rinse thoroughly, changing the water as it becomes soapy. Squeeze out the water with your hands, and swing the tail to help get rid of any remaining water. Comb through the ends gently to prevent tangles. To help the tail remain untangled, spray lightly with a show-sheen product and brush through with a body brush a few strands at a time.

Turning a Horse out for a Show

Don't wash your horse's mane the day before a show. It will be slippery and more difficult to plait. Instead, wash it a couple of days earlier so that some of the natural oils return. On the morning of the show, thoroughly wash the horse's whole body

▶ Always wash the mane thoroughly a few days before the show. Be careful not to get soap into the eyes.

and tail. Scrub hooves and socks. Make sure you dry the horse thoroughly, particularly if the weather is at all cold. First use a sweat scraper to get rid of surface water, then rub down with a towel. Plait the horse's mane and tail (see section on how to plait), and rug and bandage the horse up until you are nearly ready to go into the ring. Next, carefully apply hoof oil, and use a chalk block to make the horse's socks white. A touch of baby oil can be used to emphasize its eyes and muzzle, which should have been sponged clean first. Run a stable rubber over the coat to remove all final traces of dust, and check that the horse's plaits are still neatly in place.

Grooming Horses Which Live Outside

If an outdoor horse is rugged, the skin will become scurfy in the same way as that of a stable-kept horse, and a similar amount of regular and thorough grooming will be required. If a horse is grass-kept and *without* rugs, the skin should be in a healthy condition and it is unnecessary to groom it unless it is being ridden. In this case, grooming should be limited to:

• Picking out the feet every day and checking the shoes.
• Brushing down with the dandy brush to remove mud and sweat marks. (After exercise, do not wash down, but allow the sweat to dry, then brush it off.)
• Sponging out the eyes, nose, muzzle and dock.

Strapping

Strapping is a traditional way of improving muscle tone and development by rhythmically 'thumping' the horse's shoulders, quarters and neck with a leather massage pad, followed by 'sliding' the pad over them. It is rarely used these days except by old-fashioned horsemen and women, but done correctly it can be beneficial. It should be attempted only by people who know what they are doing, otherwise quite a lot of damage could be done. Get someone experienced to show you how to do it.

▶ A whole-body wash-down is only necessary for stable-kept horses or those entering a show.

Trimming and Plaiting

Clipping

Clipping involves removing part of the horse's winter coat with electronic clippers. It is done so that horses become less sweaty during winter work, makes grooming easier, allows horses to dry faster and means that cuts, grazes and lumps can be spotted more easily.

How to clip Introduce horses which have not been clipped before to clippers gradually. Let them become accustomed to the noise of the clippers first, and use a helper to stand at their head to reassure them. Always clip against the direction of the hair growth, and use long, sweeping strokes. Pull the skin taut over any 'fiddly' places, such as the elbows and stifle joints. Work quickly and, if the clippers become very hot, allow them to cool down before starting clipping again. Make sure that the blades are sharp and well oiled, and send the blades away to an expert to be resharpened and maintained when they become blunt.

Trimming

Trimming the excess hair from areas such as the head and legs can improve the horse's appearance. Use a pair of blunt scissors to remove unwanted hair from the coronet band at the top of the hoof and the back of the heels and fetlock joint (known as 'feather').

▶ Take care when clipping the horse's head. Some horses do not like the noise and sensation of it and will react, although the horse pictured is very relaxed.

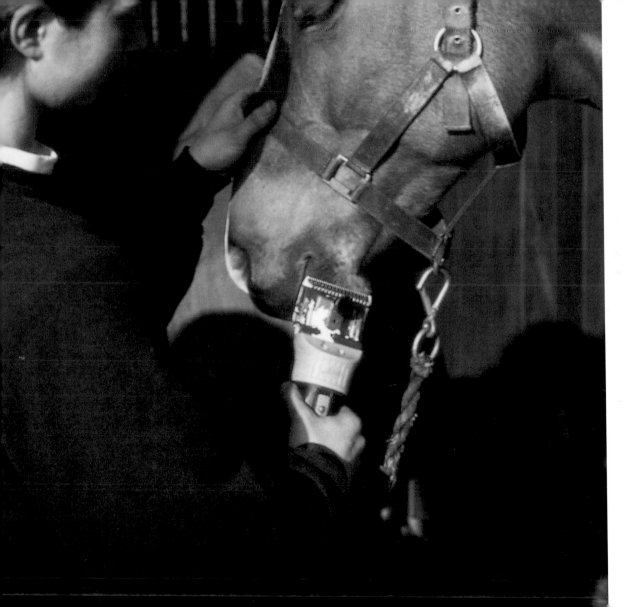

To trim the horse's 'beard' underneath its chin, either use scissors or a quiet pair of clippers. Trim close to the jawbone, and gently stretch the loose skin to achieve a neat appearance. Some people remove the horse's chin whiskers with a pair of scissors, but others believe horses need these whiskers as part of their sensory equipment.

Trim the end of a horse's tail to about 12 cm (5 in) below its hocks. This will not prevent the tail being used to whisk away flies, but will keep it out of the wintry mud.

Mane and tail pulling

Always use a comb to 'pull' tails and manes, not a pair of scissors. This achieves a more natural look. Take a small section of mane, backcomb it and tug the remainder out sharply. Do a little at a time, and it is kindest to the horse to do this after exercise, when the body is warm and the hair comes out more easily.

Plaiting

Plaiting manes and tails is done to improve a horse's appearance and make it look smart for competitions, showing and hunting.

Plaiting a mane Brush the mane and damp it down so that it lies flat. Divide the short well-pulled mane into small equal sections with rubber bands. Starting at the top, plait each section tightly and secure the bottom either with an elastic band or using needle and thread, depending on which you find easier. Roll up the plait to form a neat 'knot', and either stitch in or secure with another elastic band.

► This style of plaiting is seen more typically amongst the Spanish breeds of horse, and also for some draught breeds. It enhances the look of the topline and can only be done on horses with long manes.

Tradition used to dictate that you made either seven or nine plaits along the neck and one

at the forelock, but these days you can choose how many suits your horse – or how many it takes you to reach the end of the neck.

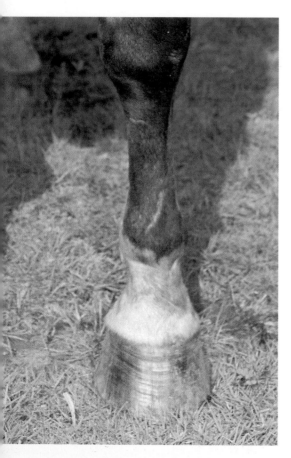

Improving the appearance of the neck Thick, chunky plaits will make the neck look shorter and bulkier; lots of small plaits will lengthen the neck and slim it down. Dressage horses often have a great number of small plaits banded with white tape, while show horses usually have bigger, more spaced-out plaits, sewn in for neatness.

Shoeing a Horse

There is a growing trend to leave horses unshod and, for certain horses, with careful hoof trimming this may be satisfactory. But for the majority of the horse population, the application of metal shoes allows them to do the work expected of them. The art of shoeing horses is called 'farriery', and the person who shoes your horse is a 'farrier'. Each horse's hooves are different, and it is important to find a farrier who will take time to understand what your horse needs.

◄ Leaving a horse unshod should only be done, with careful hoof trimming, on horses of whom little work is expected.

► Metal studs can be fitted into the heel of a shoe to lessen the risk of slipping. It is preferable to use one on the inside and one on the outside of each shoe, to maintain the balance of the hoof.

The Structure of the Hoof

The exterior is made up of three parts: the wall, the sole and the frog (*see also* page 30–33). All three are non-sensitive and contain neither nerves nor blood, which is why nails can be driven through the wall and why the frog and wall can be trimmed back without causing pain or bleeding.

The wall This is the part of the hoof visible when the foot is on the ground. It grows downwards from the coronet, like a fingernail.

The sole This thin structure protects the hoof from injury from underneath, and is slightly concave, to provide grip.

The frog This wedge-shaped structure grows downwards from the heel on the underside of the horse's hoof. It is the horse's anti-slipping and anti-concussion pad, and should be flexible and cushion-like.

How Often Should My Horse Be Shod?

Most horses will need shoeing every four to six weeks, depending on how quickly their hooves grow and how much work they are doing. Even when the shoes are not badly worn, the hoof will have grown and needs trimming.

Signs That a Horse Needs Shoeing

- The foot is long and out of shape.
- The shoe has worn thin.
- The shoe is loose or has come off.
- The 'clenches' (the nail heads that protrude from the hoof wall) have risen and stand out.

▶ These farrier's tools are, from left to right, buffer, hoof cutters, rasp, shoeing hammer and drawing knife.

The Farrier's Visit

Before your farrier arrives, make sure that your horse's legs and feet are clean and dry, and that it is standing in a suitably sheltered place, preferably with a flat, clean surface.

To remove a shoe, the farrier cuts all the clenches, using a buffer and driving hammer. He then levers the shoe off with pincers. The overgrowth of hoof wall is removed with a drawing knife, and ragged parts of the sole and frog are trimmed away. A rasp is then used to give the foot a level bearing surface.

The new, hot shoe is then taken to the hoof on a pritchel and seared to the hoof to check that the shoe fits the shape of the foot. After any adjustments, the shoe is cooled in water and nailed on. The first nail is usually driven into the toe, and outwards from there.

The end of the nail, where it penetrates from the wall, is turned over and twisted off, leaving a small 'clench'. The clenches are tidied up with the rasp, and the toe-clip tapped lightly back into position.

The Newly Shod Foot

Check that:

- The shoe has been made to fit the hoof, not the hoof made to fit the shoe.
- The type and weight of the shoe is suitable for the horse.
- The frog has been correctly trimmed: it should make contact with the ground on soft surfaces, as its role is as a concussion pad.
- No daylight shows between the shoe and the hoof, particularly at the heel region.
- The heels of the shoe are neither too long nor too short.

▶ The cooled shoe is nailed on by the farrier, starting at the toe.

Health

Keeping a horse healthy means constant vigilance. The horse cannot tell you if something is wrong, so your perception and assessment of its condition are vital to its wellbeing. You will also need to take certain active steps to maintain your horse's health, such as worming. Learn what is and isn't normal for your horse, and maintain a weather eye for any signs of deterioration or change. Any deviations from the signs of good health listed below should be noted and appropriate action taken as quickly as possible.

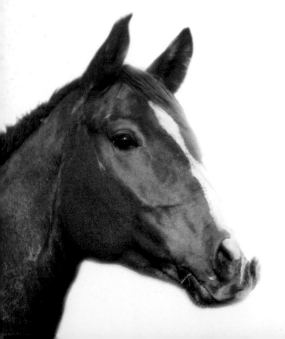

Signs of Good Health

- The horse should be standing and behaving normally.
- It should be alert and confident.
- There should be no signs of sweating at rest, except in very hot weather.
- Its eyes should be bright and wide open.
- The membranes under the eyelids and the linings of the nostrils should be salmon pink in colour.
- It should be eating well and chewing normally.
- Its coat should be sleek and lying flat, not dull and 'stary'.

▶ The horse in this picture is a good example of a horse in good health. The coat is shiny, ears pricked and eyes alert.

- Its limbs should be free from heat and swellings.
- It should be standing evenly on all four feet. Resting a hindleg is quite normal; resting a front leg is a cause for concern.
- Its urine and droppings should be normal in colour and passed at the normal rate. Horses fed on hay will pass light-coloured, yellow-brown droppings, while those at grass will pass dark green droppings.
- The skin should move easily over the horse's ribs, which should neither be too visible nor obscured by excess fat.
- At rest, the horse's temperature should be within the range 37°–38.5°C (99.5°–101.3°F).
- At rest, the horse's respiration (breathing) rate should be 10 to 20 inhalations per minute.
- At rest, the horse's pulse should be 36 to 42 heartbeats per minute.

Routine Healthcare

Vaccination

All horses must be vaccinated against tetanus, which is a serious disease, picked up from bacteria in soil, that can result in death. If you do not know the vaccination history of your horse, it must have an initial course of injections, then a booster every year.

◄ Horses should always be vaccinated against tetanus, and sometimes against flu.

► Worming treatment usually comes as a paste that can be orally syringed.

Flu vaccinations are optional but recommended, and are compulsory if you wish to compete at affiliated level in any discipline. The course consists of an initial injection, a second one between 21 and 90 days later, a third one between 115 and 210 days after the second, and annual boosters afterwards. These need to be six-monthly if you are competing under International Equestrian Federation (FEI) rules.

Always ensure that your horse's vaccinations are up to date. If they lapse, you will have to start all over again.

Worming

All horses and ponies can suffer from worms, caused by ingesting immature larvae while grazing. It is important to control these worms, through pasture management and a worming programme.

Droppings should be picked up from pasture or, if the field is too big to make this practical, have the field harrowed so that the droppings are broken up and spread. Do not graze horses with donkeys, as the latter pass on lungworms.

Wormers usually come in the form of a paste, which can be 'injected' into the mouth so that the horse eats it. Take advice from your vet about a suitable worming programme; there are different types of wormers to combat different worms. On average, horses should be wormed every six to eight weeks.

Teeth

It is good practice to have your horse's teeth checked at least once a year, either by your vet or a qualified horse dentist. Some horses will never need anything done to their teeth, while others may need regular treatment and rasping for sharp edges and uneven wear.

► This horse is wearing a speculum, or mouth gag, which keeps the mouth open, allowing the dentist to work on the teeth more efficiently.

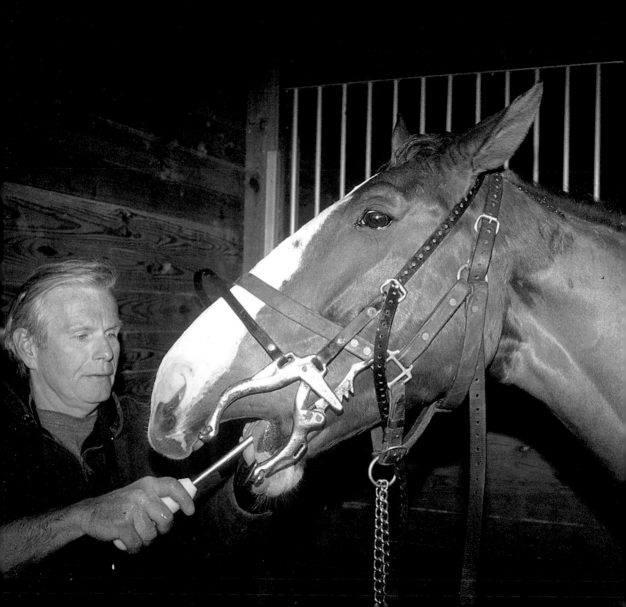

First Aid and Wounds

There are several different types of wound. Some you will be able to manage yourself, but others will need veterinary attention. If in any doubt, call the vet. It is better to be safe than sorry. Keep the vet's phone number to hand to minimize delays.

Minor Wounds

Superficial grazes, scrapes and small cuts can be managed by clipping away the surrounding hair and cleaning thoroughly. To wash the wound, use a mild antiseptic solution in warm, clean water from a clean bucket. If you do not have antiseptic handy, kitchen salt will suffice. Soak pads of cotton wool in the water and gently rub the wound, changing the cotton wool frequently.

Do not apply a wound ointment or powder because these make dirt stick and attract infection. If possible, apply a non-stick dressing, then bandage. Keep the horse in a stable, if possible, because it is easier to keep the wound clean. Check the horse's tetanus vaccinations are up to date.

When to Call the Vet

Always call a qualified veterinarian in the following situations:

- If blood is spurting from the wound.
- If the wound is to the foot, over a joint or near a tendon, or to the eye. Infection in the foot is difficult to treat once established. Wounds near joints are dangerous because of the risk of joint oil (synovial fluid) leaking out of the joint capsule and serious infection resulting. If a horse falls over on the road and damages its knees, seek veterinary advice, however superficial the injury may look.

▶ Wash minor wounds in warm, clean water with antiseptic or salt.

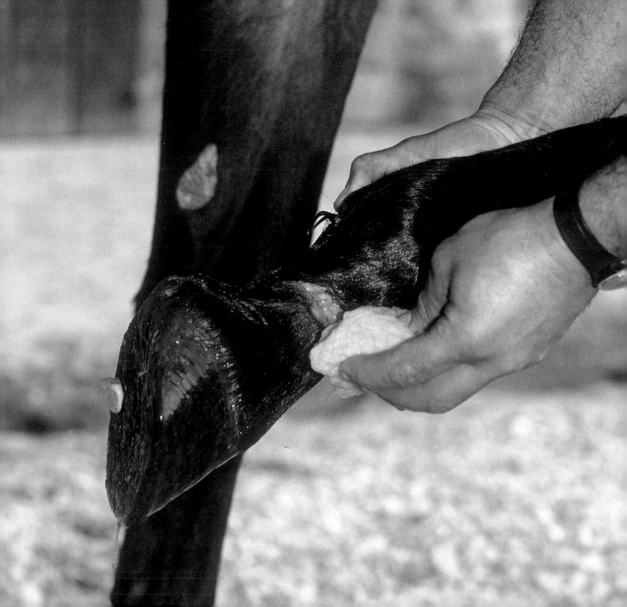

- If the cut is big enough to need stitching, whether it is jagged-edged or clean-edged.
- If the horse has picked up a puncture wound. This is a small, deep wound, perhaps from a nail or sharp pointed object. The danger is that they are easy to miss and, because of their depth, may have damaged the internal structures of the horse or contain foreign bodies and dirt that you cannot see. They are difficult to clean out, and may need poulticing.

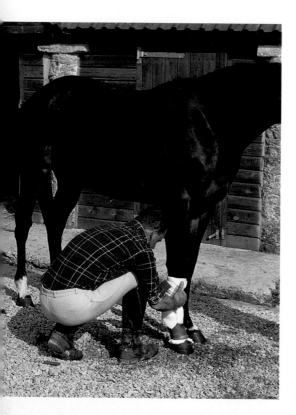

If you have called the vet in an emergency, there are a few things you can do to help the situation. If blood is spurting, push a clean pad of cotton wool into the wound, and either hold or bandage into place.

With all major wounds, try to prevent the horse from panicking or moving too much, so that further damage is minimized. Make sure that you have warm water and some clean towels ready.

Deep wounds, where the blood is not spurting out, can be liberally hosed with cold water until the vet arrives. This will constrict the blood vessels and help to stop the bleeding.

◄ While waiting for the vet, maintain pressure on a spurting wound with a clean cotton wool pad, which can be held in place with a bandage.

► Cold hosing is an excellent therapy for any type of bruising injury on the legs or feet, and helps to reduce inflammation.

Girth Galls and Saddle Sores

If a horse's tack does not fit properly, it will rub and cause a sore patch. Wash the area with a weak antiseptic solution, and, when the skin has healed, harden it up with surgical spirit. Most importantly, discover what is rubbing and take steps to prevent it. A fleece girth-guard should be used until the problem is solved. For saddle sores, do not ride the horse until they are completely healed, and seek the advice of a saddle-fitter.

Mouth Injuries

Badly fitting bits, or those with sharp or worn edges, can damage the mouth, particularly if combined with rough riding. Cracks to the corners of the mouth are most common, which can become very sore. Check the bit for damage or pinching, and change it accordingly. Applying calendula cream, or haemorrhoid cream formulated for humans, will help to heal the sores. In bad cases, you may have to refrain from using a bit for some days.

▲ Girth galls such as this pictured can quickly become open sores if they are not noticed. They must be allowed to completely heal before the horse is saddled again, and the girth should be changed.

▶ If the horse's mouth has been damaged by the bit, the horse can wear a bitless bridle while it recovers.

Signs of Ill Health

Common signs of illness include:

- Dullness and depression
- Failure to eat and sudden weight loss
- A dull and 'stary' coat
- Patchy sweating at rest
- Box-walking and general unease
- Getting up and lying down repeatedly
- Ears laid back
- Runny, weeping eyes
- A running nose
- Abnormal pulse and respiration rates
- A raised temperature
- Swelling or heat in a leg
- Resting a foreleg, or shifting constantly from one leg to another
- Lameness
- Drinking and urinating more than normal
- Patchy hair loss
- Discoloured droppings and urine, or droppings of an unusual consistency
- Coughing
- Skin lumps
- Aggression towards other horses or humans
- Disinclination to socialize with other horsesin the field
- Poor performance and poor exercise tolerance

▲ Weight and hair loss are clear signs of ill health.

▶ Whenever a horse rests or 'points' a front leg, as seen here, it indicates pain in the limb and should be investigated immediately.

It is important to know what is 'normal' for your horse, particularly in terms of respiration, pulse rates and temperature.

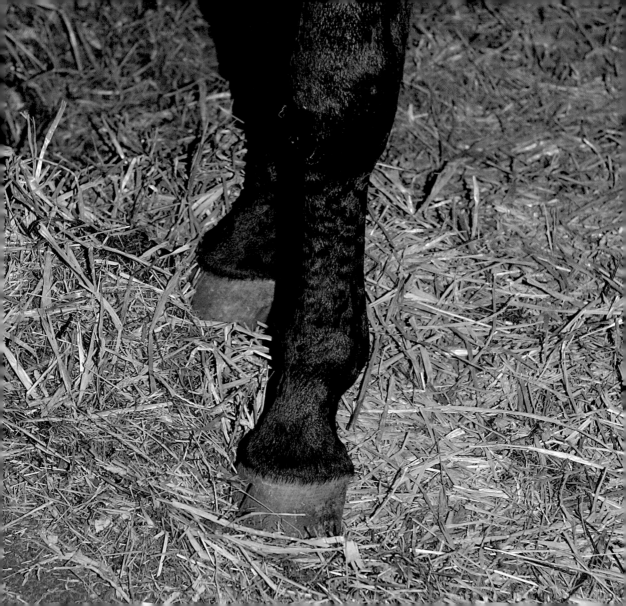

Taking Your Horse's Temperature

Grease the bulb of a thermometer, preferably a digital one, and gently insert it into the horse's rectum. Do not stand directly behind the horse in case it kicks, and hold the tail out of the way. Hold on to the thermometer firmly (plenty of these have been lost inside horses, which necessitates a visit to the vet), and leave for two minutes, or until it bleeps if it is digital. Withdraw the thermometer and read the temperature. Make sure that you wash the thermometer thoroughly.

Taking the Pulse Rate

The easiest places to feel the pulse are where the facial artery crosses the jawbone and just below the horse's elbow. Make sure that you take the pulse rate with your fingers, not your thumb, which has a pulse of its own. Count the number of pulses in 15 seconds, and multiply by four to get a reading.

Taking the Respiration Rate

Watch the horse's flanks move in and out, and count for a minute. Breathing should be regular and quiet.

◄ Take the pulse rate with your finger, not your thumb.

► This horse is displaying a classic laminitic stance, with its weight rocked back onto its hindquarters and front legs stretched out. This is to reduce the stress on the painful front feet.

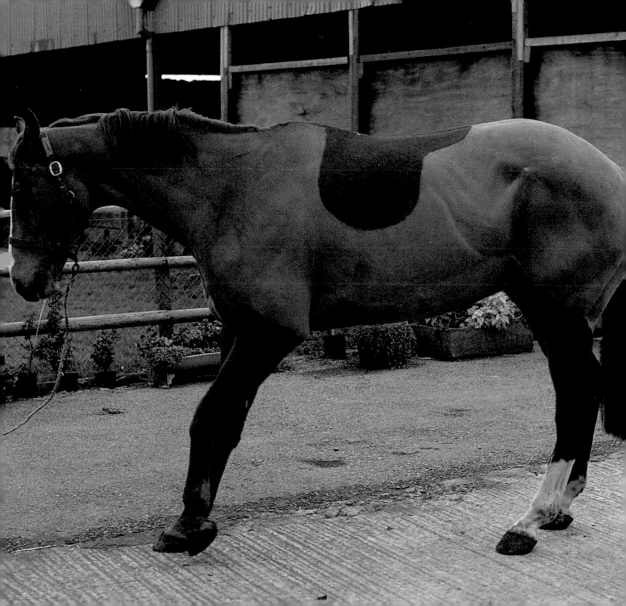

Common Ailments and Treatment

All horse owners should possess a basic first-aid box containing the following:

- Cotton wool
- Blunt-ended scissors
- A thermometer
- Antiseptic solution for cleaning wounds
- A variety of different-sized dressings
- Surgical tape
- Gamgee tissue
- A selection of bandages
- Self-adhesive bandage, such as Vetwrap
- Animalintex or similar impregnated multi-layered poultice
- Epsom salts
- a clean bowl or small bucket
- Vaseline
- Your vet's and farrier's phone numbers

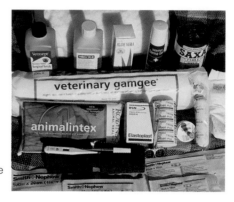

▶ This is a pony suffering from chronic laminitis. The farrier has trimmed the hoof away at the toe area to relieve the pressure, and therefore pain, and to encourage new horn to grow.

Lameness

Many horse owners will have to cope with some degree of lameness in their horse at some point. It can range from mild to severe, and be sudden in onset or gradual. If both forelegs or both hindlegs, or all four legs, are affected, it can be difficult to detect because there may not be an obvious limp; the stride length may just be shorter or the horse may be unwilling to go forwards freely.

Nearly all lameness is a result of foot pain (the most common reason) or damage to the leg's soft structures, such as tendons and ligaments.

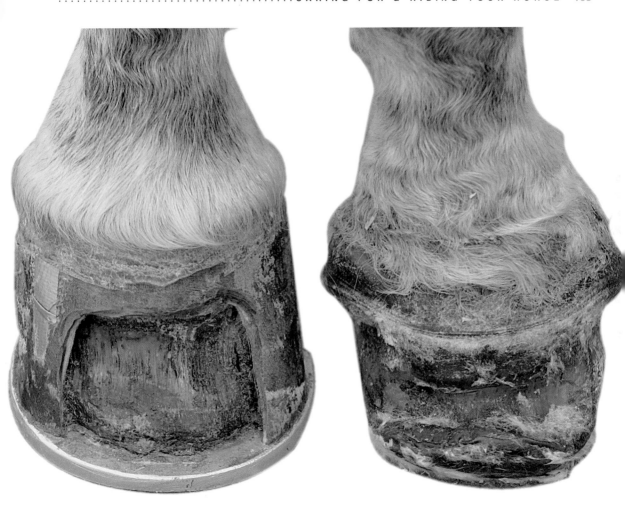

Laminitis

Laminitis is a painful condition of the feet, caused by inflammation of the laminae, which are sensitive membranes on the inside of the hoof wall. It can affect any horse at any time of the year, but is particularly prevalent in small ponies, especially natives, in the spring. It has many causes, but the most common is carbohydrate overload from too much rich food, particularly grass. Others include insulin resistance, too much work on hard ground, infection, lameness resulting in hoof imbalance, a hormonal disease called Cushing's, or reactions to certain drugs such as corticosteroids.

The hoof wall is hot to the touch, with an increased digital pulse. The horse will stand with its weight tipped back on to its heels, and will be unwilling to move. Horses with a severe case of laminitis may lie down and refuse to get up.

Treatment Call the vet. In the meantime, make the horse as comfortable as possible. Do not remove all access to food and water, and do not hose the horse's feet in an effort to reduce the heat.

Other Sources of Foot Pain

Other forms of lameness in the foot may be the result of abscesses, where infection has built up and can cause the horse to be severely lame. Veterinary treatment will be needed to drain the abscess. Corns or bruises at the heel between the frog and the hoof wall are fairly common and are often the result of ill-fitting shoes. Stones can become lodged in the foot and will make a horse instantly lame. Thrush is a smelly fungal infection of the underside of the foot, with a black discharge oozing from the frog. Bad stable management or poor foot care is the usual cause.

▶ Ponies that are susceptible to laminitis should have their grazing carefully monitored. Lush green grass such as that pictured can trigger laminitis, especially in overweight ponies.

Tendon and Ligament Damage

The flexor tendons and check and suspensory ligaments at the back of the horse's lower leg are vulnerable and liable to damage because of the amount of strain they take when a horse moves. Some injuries to these do not initially cause lameness, only some heat and swelling. If you suspect damage, rest the horse immediately and call the vet. It is very difficult for the layperson to tell how severe these injuries are without expert advice. Early identification and treatment can make all the difference to recovery.

Skin Diseases

Most skin diseases are not serious and are relatively easy to treat. But they can be infectious and spread to other horses, and even people, so prompt and efficient management is vital.

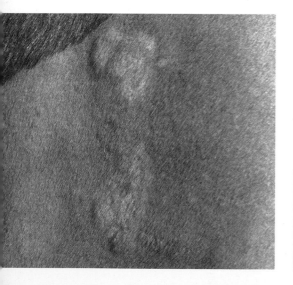

Ringworm This is not caused by a worm at all, but is a fungal infection that affects the roots of the hair. It is identified by small round bare patches, and is highly infectious to other horses and humans. The horse should be isolated, and all tack, rugs and grooming kit must be thoroughly cleaned and kept separate from that belonging to other horses. Wash your hands and exposed skin after attending to the affected horse to minimize the risk of cross-infection.

▶ Despite the hardy appearance of horse's legs, they are susceptible to injury, especially tendon and ligament strain.

◀ Ringworm manifests as small, round, bare patches, as seen here, although sometimes the lesions will exude a thick serum. It is a highly contagious condition, and can be caught by humans.

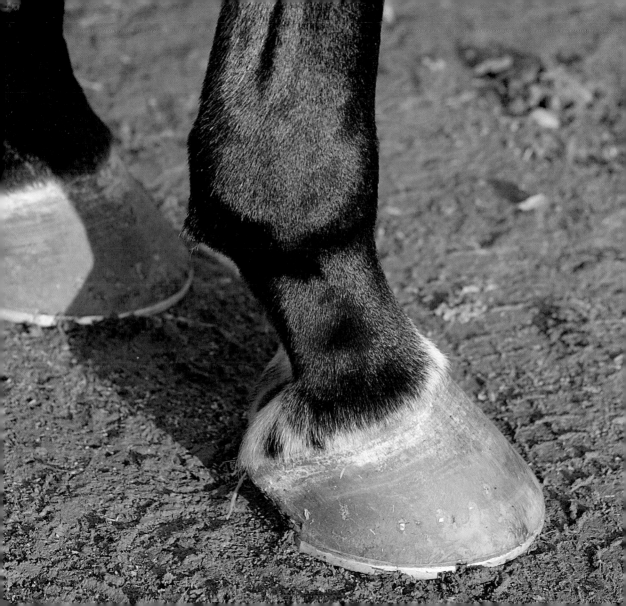

Sweet itch This is an unpleasant condition caused by an allergy to midge bites, and causes severe itchiness around the mane and tail. It affects ponies more frequently than horses, and drives them to rub themselves raw. It is incurable, but can be kept under control through careful management. It is helpful to keep the animal in the stable at dawn and dusk, when the midges are at their worst, and fly repellent should be used liberally. There are also some specially designed rugs which have proved highly effective, made of light cloth which tightly covers the horse from nose to tail.

Mud fever Many horses suffer from mud fever at one time or another. When the skin surrounding the heels and the lower leg is softened by damp, bacteria enter the skin and infection develops. The skin becomes lumpy and cracked, and may weep yellowy fluid. The horse's legs may swell up, and it can become very painful. Horses get it from standing in wet conditions and mud, and it can be prevented by keeping their legs clean and dry, or covering the legs with grease or baby oil before turning them out. Wash mud off when they are brought in after turn-out or exercise, then dry thoroughly. To treat, trim the hair back to help keep the legs clean and dry. Your vet will advise you on antibacterial creams to heal the infection.

Colic

Colic means abdominal pain, and has an almost infinite number of causes and levels of severity, from mild to life-threatening. Always call the vet if you suspect your horse has colic, as early treatment is essential and surgery may be required.

◄ If a horse keeps getting up and down it may be a sign of colic.

► Mud fever is a painful condition that is commonly seen on the lower limbs, but can also be present underneath of the belly.

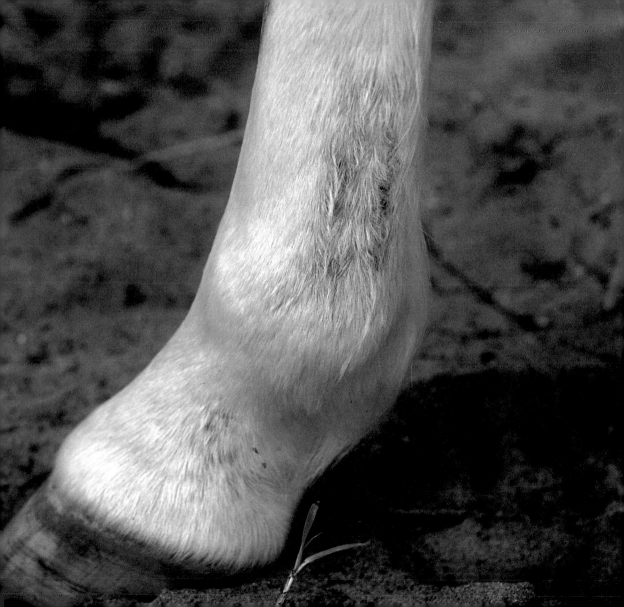

Symptoms of colic The horse will look uncomfortable and uneasy, and kick at its belly. There may be patchy sweating, and its heart, temperature and respiration rates may be increased. Other signs are a failure to eat up, not passing droppings as normal, and getting up and down.

Action While you are waiting for the vet, try to keep the horse as calm as possible. It may be severely distressed and potentially dangerous; if this is the case, do not interfere. But if it is calm, remove any feed or hay from the stable, and note if any droppings have been passed. If the horse wishes to lie down, let it, but prevent it from rolling if you can. The vet will assess the severity of the problem, identify the type of colic and treat accordingly.

Some causes of colic:

- Bolting food
- Ingesting sand from a stream or sandy ground
- Working hard too close to a meal time
- Worms
- Sudden changes in diet
- Poor tooth care
- Mouldy hay or hard food
- Drinking too much cold water immediately after exercise

◄ Do not diagnose the condition yourself. Wait for the vet to check your horse thoroughly.

► Poor teeth can be a cause of colic.

Fitness Regimes and Training

How fit your horse needs to be will depend on what you wish to do with it, but the fitter the horse is, the easier it will find it to work, and the less risk there is of doing damage to its joints, muscles, tendons and ligaments.

Basic Fitness Programme

This plan assumes that you are starting with a totally unfit horse, but one that is in good condition. Horses in poor condition will take longer to get fit and will find it much harder. It would be better to spend some time improving the horse's condition before attempting to work it. Allow 12 to 14 weeks to get your horse fit enough for hard work, such as horse trials, hunting or any form of exercise that requires considerable exertion.

▲ Lungeing is a good basic form of exercise and training (*see* page 206).

▶ The walk phase of the regime is the most important. It is the building block for the work to come.

Before you start

- Check that the horse's worming and vaccination programmes are up to date.
- Check that its teeth are in good condition and don't need rasping, and organize for the farrier to visit and shoe the horse if necessary.
- Trim and tidy up the horse's mane, tail and heels.

First stage

- Stay in walk, including road work, for at least three weeks. Start with 30 minutes a day, building up to an hour and a half.
- If the horse is returning from an injury, extend the walking period to six weeks.

- Make sure that the horse walks out in an active manner and in balance; slopping along with the reins swinging will not help to get the animal fit and muscled up.

Second stage

- Combine walking with slow trotting for another three weeks, building the exercise up to two hours six days a week if possible. Use hillwork to build up muscle.
- Some steady trotting on good roads helps to harden the legs, but do not overdo it, as it can make them jar.
- You can also introduce some schooling on the flat, some slow cantering for short periods and, towards the end of the six weeks, some simple jumping.

Third stage

- By this time, the horse should be ready to improve its respiratory fitness as well as its muscular fitness. Find some open ground with good going, and start with a quarter of a mile of cantering interspersed with trotting. Build up the distance gradually until the horse is cantering for a mile at a good, controlled pace, once or twice a week.
- Slow work up a hill is beneficial; hillwork enables you to do shorter, sharper pieces of work with your horse without putting unnecessary strain on its legs by working for long periods of time.
- Hacking, schooling and gymnastic jumping should be done on the other days of the week.

▶ Trot work, especially on a hill, as seen here is important for building up stamina and strength.

Interval Training

Interval training is a useful refinement of your basic fitness regime, and can be included in the final two weeks of the programme. It is designed to strengthen the horse's muscles and respiratory system by a gradual increase in 'stress', and consists of repeated spells of canter interspersed with periods of walk in which the horse is allowed almost, but not quite, to recover its pre-work pulse rate before going on to the next interval of fast work. Not allowing the pulse to drop completely strengthens the heart, lungs and muscles, and helps them to adapt to the stress placed on them. It also develops the capacity of the horse's respiratory and circulatory systems.

As an example, a horse getting fit for a novice-level one-day event would canter for three minutes, walk for three minutes, and canter again for three minutes, increasing the canter periods depending on how much fitter you wish the horse to become.

You must be practical: tailor your horse's fitness programme to suit the time you have available and your facilities. Not everyone has a hill to work up, or good hacking. Cantering the horse in balance round and round the school on each rein can, if done properly, be just as good if it is your only option.

▲ ► Keep the horse's work schedule interesting by interspersing hacking out with school work and jumping.

Rider Fitness

Riders are increasingly aware of the need to be fit to ride. Fitness is important because a lack of fitness for a

specific activity results in early fatigue, which leads to a failure of skill and an increase in the risk of injury. If you 'hit the wall' and get very tired halfway round a cross-country course, you effectively become a passenger and cannot help the horse when it needs it. We all want to ride our horses to the best of our abilities, and being unfit makes you a less effective, less balanced rider. It also increases your risk of injury and your risk of falling off. Even if you don't want to compete, getting fitter can help you stay safe and injury-free.

Fitness can be divided into stamina, strength and suppleness. Stamina strengthens your heart and lungs, strength tones your muscles to allow you to do physical work without injury, and suppleness enhances mobility. For general fitness and non-competitive riding, a balance of all three is best. Depending on your riding discipline and how well schooled your horse is, suppleness and stamina are probably the most important, followed by strength. Stamina becomes more important the longer the duration of your discipline; endurance riding requires higher levels of stamina than dressage. Jockeys riding in races and event riders have to have a far higher amount of strength than endurance riders or dressage competitors.

◄ It is important for the rider to be fit as well as the horse. Otherwise, it adds to the burden on the horse, especially when jumping.

► Always wash the horse down after work to remove traces of sweat from the coat and to cool him down.

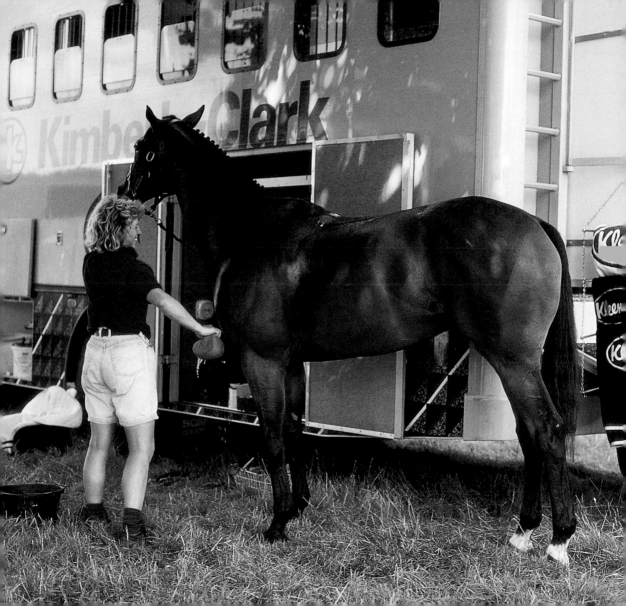

Riding and Training

Riding is the reason most of us own a horse. Achieving harmony and understanding between horse and rider may be a long, slow process, but it is the aim of all who ride and worth working hard to reach. Good instruction from a qualified teacher who you find easy to understand and who truly wishes to help you improve is extremely valuable. Don't be afraid to 'try out' a few instructors in an effort to find the one with whom you click best, and be clear about what you want to achieve.

Riding Gear

The most essential part of your riding gear is a hard hat that complies with the most recent safety standards. It is better to sacrifice elegance for comfort and safety than to compromise your head, and hats should be fitted with a chin strap. Appropriate boots should be worn; these should have a heel, to prevent the foot from slipping through the stirrup. Short boots are more comfortable if worn with half-chaps to protect the lower leg. Trainers and athletic shoes are *not* suitable.

It is a good idea to wear gloves when riding, even in the summer, to help prevent blisters and rubs. Jodhpurs or breeches are the best clothing for your legs, but many people ride happily in jeans or tracksuit trousers if just hacking. Hacking jackets are best kept for competitions and hunting. Clothing should be comfortable, and close-fitting enough to avoid restricting movement or becoming entwined in tack.

▶ A hard hat is the most important element of your riding gear. Wear jackets that don't restrict movement, and gloves are a good idea.

The Paces

The horse has four basic paces: walk, trot, canter and gallop. At all paces, the rider should be in balance and harmony with the horse, and the horse should be going in a balanced, rhythmical manner.

Walk

This is a four-time gait, and should be purposeful and regular. The sequence of footfalls is: left hind, left fore, right hind, right fore. The horse always has two feet on the ground at the same time.

Trot

The trot is a diagonal two-time pace, with two beats to a stride. The sequence of footfalls is: left hind and right fore together, then right hind and left fore together, with a moment of suspension, when all four feet are above the ground, in between.

Canter

The canter is a three-time pace with three beats to the stride. When the left foreleg is leading, the sequence is: right hind, then left hind and right fore together, then left fore. The leading leg is always last. When the right foreleg is leading, the sequence is: left hind, then right hind and left fore together, then lastly right fore. There is a moment of suspension after the leading leg touches the ground.

◄ ► The walk (left) is a four-beat gait, while the trot (right) is two-time.

Gallop

This is the fastest pace of the horse, and a proper gallop (instead of a speedy canter) is a four-time movement. The sequence of legs with the left fore leading is: right hind, left hind, right fore and lastly the leading leg, the left fore, followed by a moment of suspension when all four legs are off the ground. The sequence of footfalls with the right fore leading is: left hind, right hind, left fore, and lastly the right fore, followed by a moment of suspension.

When a horse is going in the correct way in all four basic paces, it is time to move on to more advanced work. This can include changes within the individual paces: collection and extension. In collected paces (walk, trot and canter), the rhythm and tempo remain the same, but greater activity is shown. Each step is higher and shorter, covering less ground, and the speed is thus decreased. Extension (extended walk, trot and canter) is the opposite; again, the rhythm and tempo remain consistent, but the horse covers more ground with each stride without hurrying and losing the regularity. Both require more impulsion (controlled energy) than the basic paces.

The Basics

Mounting and Dismounting

- Before you can ride your horse, you have to get on it. Check the girth is tight enough to ensure that the saddle will not slip round. Pull the stirrup irons down, and check the stirrup length is approximately right. To do this, pull the stirrup leathers down, put your hand at the top near the buckle and lift up the stirrup iron. It should approximately reach your armpit.

▶ The canter is a three-beat gait. A good canter should maintain a steady and even rhythm with propulsion coming from the hindquarters.

- We generally mount from the 'near side' (the left), but it is important to be able to do so equally well from both sides. Stand with your left shoulder to the horse's left shoulder, and take the reins into the left hand, which should then be placed in front of the withers. Put your left foot into the stirrup iron, and pivot to face the horse. Place your right hand at the back of the saddle, and spring lightly up, taking care to lower yourself into the saddle and not to land heavily on the horse's back. Put your right foot into the stirrup, and quietly gather up the reins in both hands. Although everybody should be able to mount from the ground, it is in fact often better for the horse's back to use a mounting block.

- It is equally important to be able to dismount from both sides, and the horse should be used to you doing this. But usually we dismount from the near side. Remove both feet from the stirrups, and gather the reins in the left hand. Put your left hand on the horse's neck, and lean forwards. Swing your right leg back over the horse's hindquarters, allowing both feet to slip to the ground. Bend your knees and land lightly, clear of the horse.

- Do not swing your leg over the front of the saddle and jump off facing outwards. This is dangerous because, if the horse moves while you are getting off, you can fall down and land flat on your back with your head near the horse's front feet.

- **Adjusting the girth and stirrups while mounted** It is important to be able to change the length of your stirrups and to tighten or loosen your girth without getting off. To alter the right stirrup, do not take your feet out of the stirrups, but draw up your leg, hold the reins in the left hand and use the other hand to adjust the stirrup leather. To adjust the girth on the left-hand side, hold the reins in your right hand, and put your leg forward over the knee rolls of the saddle. Lift up the saddle flap and adjust each girth strap as necessary, taking care not to pinch the horse and that the buckle guards are lying flat over the girth buckles. Ideally, the girth buckles should be at the same height on the girth straps on both sides of the saddle.

▶ When mounting place your left foot in the nearside stirrup and your right hand to the back of the saddle, jump and land lightly and fluidly in the saddle. A mounting block is better for the horse's back.

The Rider's Position

The rider should sit squarely in the saddle, at the lowest part. You should feel your seatbones are carrying equal amounts of weight on each side, and your back should be straight. Don't be tempted to sit rigidly upright; your whole body should be supple and without tension, with the seat, thighs and knees lying relaxed and straight. The ball of the foot should rest on the bar of the stirrup iron, with the natural drop of the rider's weight keeping it in place. The rider's ear, shoulder, hip and heel should form a straight line, and another straight line should pass from the rider's elbow through to the hand and along the rein to the horse's mouth.

Holding the reins

To carry the reins correctly, they come from the horse's mouth through the rider's third finger and little finger across the palm and over the index finger, with the thumb on top. It is important that the third finger holds the edges of the rein in the joints nearest the palm and that the fingers are closed securely, but without tension.

◄ Check your stirrup length before starting to work the horse, and alter them as seen, pulling the leather upwards to release the buckle and finding a different hole to set them at, if necessary.

► This rider is sitting in a good position, her weight is centred over the horse, her legs are hanging correctly and are relaxed, and her back is nice and straight.

When holding two reins – for example, if you are using a double bridle – hold as for the single rein, except that the little finger of each hand should divide the reins. The bridoon rein is usually held on the outside.

Contact

This refers to the relationship between a rider's hands and the horse's mouth, down the reins. It is important to be able to move your hands independently of the rest of your body, and to keep them still and soft despite other parts of your body being in motion. When you take up the reins, you should feel some weight in your hands. This consistent weight, which should be flexible and soft, but ever present, should stay the same at all times and at all paces. The horse should accept this consistent contact happily, but will do so only if the rider is in harmony with the horse, responsive and can 'go with' the movements of the horse's head and neck without tightening or dropping the contact.

The hands should be carried with the thumbs uppermost and the backs of the hands facing outwards. Wrists should neither be floppy nor too stiff.

◄ This rider is in a poor position. Her hands are tense and pressed in a restrictive manner down onto the horse's neck, and she is stiff and tense through her whole body, including her hunched back and her legs.

► This rider is holding the reins correctly and is beginning to establish a contact.

Movement

Riders must learn to position themselves correctly at all paces, and to stay balanced and in harmony with the horse at all times. The more supple and flexible a rider is, the better that person will learn to ride.

At Walk

The only difference between the rider's position at halt and at walk is that the body moves slightly at the hips and waist in rhythm with the horse's natural movements, and the elbow and shoulder joints move to allow the rider's hand to follow the movements of the horse's head and neck.

At Trot

In rising trot, the rider rises from the saddle for one beat and sits in the saddle for the alternate beat (also called 'posting'). The rider's shoulders should lead the movement, in order to stay in balance, without tipping forwards and allowing the weight to come forwards on to the horse's shoulders. The back should remain straight; do not allow your body to collapse at the waist. Keep an even weight in the stirrups, and keep the stirrups on the ball of your foot. Try to maintain a steady and even contact on the reins. Learning to trot is probably the hardest part of learning to ride; walk and canter are much easier, but practice makes perfect.

At Canter

At canter, the rider's weight usually stays in the saddle. Supple hips are important to absorb the movement of the three-time beat, and the upper body should move in rhythm with the horse. If the rider tenses his back, he will bump in the saddle and the experience will be uncomfortable for both horse and rider.

▶ Rising trot travelling on the right rein. The rider should rise as the horse's outside shoulder moves forward, and sit as it moves back.

At Gallop

At gallop, the rider should carry her weight out of the saddle and on to the knees and stirrups. The reins and stirrup leathers will need to be shortened to allow this. The upper body should be inclined forwards, but with the weight posed over the centre of gravity. Balance is essential.

The Aids

The aids are how the rider communicates with the horse, and are divided into 'natural' aids and 'artificial' aids.

Natural Aids

The legs These are used to encourage the horse, and to ask the horse to change pace and direction. The inside leg asks for impulsion (energy) from the horse, and to encourage it to bend correctly. The outside leg controls the hindquarters.

The hands These should keep an even contact with the horse's mouth at all times. They are the principal methods of communication and should be used carefully. The inside hand is used for direction, while the outside hand controls and regulates the speed and pace, and controls bend. Used in conjunction with the legs, they are also your 'brakes'. All movements of the hands should be subtle and clear: remember that you are asking a question via a very sensitive part of the body, i.e. the mouth.

The voice This is a useful aid, particularly in training the young horse and when used in conjunction with the other aids. It is also used to reward the horse, praise it, soothe it or, if necessary, reprimand it.

▶ This horse is wearing a running martingale, and the rider is carrying a long schooling whip, which should only be used lightly.

Artificial Aids

The whip is used to teach respect for the rider's leg aid, or to correct the horse. But take care never to use it in anger. It is almost always because the horse does not understand that it disobeys; this is your fault, not the horse's. It can be useful to reinforce the leg aid if the horse does not respond, and to keep its mind on the job, by way of a quick tap behind the leg. Never hit a horse on the head or any other sensitive part of his body.

Spurs are made of metal, and fit around the rider's heel. The short shank at the point of the heel can be used to give a more refined leg aid, and should be used only by experienced riders.

Basic Manoeuvres

Changing Pace

To change pace up, or increase speed, make sure that the quality of the pace you are in is as good as possible. Sit softly in the saddle, and give a firm nudge with the legs, while avoiding restricting forward movement with the hands. To ask for canter, balance the horse in trot, sit for a few strides, bring the outside leg back behind the girth while keeping the inside leg on the girth, and give

◄ Whips are best used by experienced riders.

▶ The rider is guiding this horse around a circle. The horse and rider should remain in balance while moving round a circle.

the horse a firm nudge with the outside leg. Keep the contact constant and avoid leaning forwards. To change down a pace, or decrease speed, maintain a good contact, keep the leg on to ensure impulsion is not lost, and ask the horse to slow down with a light 'pull' on the reins.

The Halt

The halt should be 'square', i.e. the horse is standing still and straight with its weight balanced equally over all four legs. To ask for halt, repeat the instructions to decrease pace, but make the aid a little firmer and remember to use the leg as well as the hand. Never tug sharply at the horse's mouth or fail to prepare the horse for the transition.

Turns and Circles

When circling or turning, the rider wants the horse's body to bend equally from poll to tail. Make sure that you resist the temptation to twist your own body; keep the hips and shoulders parallel to those of the horse, and turn your head only to indicate the direction you want to take. Your inside hand controls the direction, so ask the horse to turn with a firm but sympathetic aid. Keep the outside hand back to control the pace and stop the horse's neck from bending too much without its body following. The outside leg stays on the girth, while the inside leg may nudge the horse to encourage the horse to change direction and bend.

Jumping

Rider Position

To jump successfully, riders need to shorten their stirrup leathers by a couple of holes. This closes the angles at the knees and ankles, which should help give you a balanced and

▶ This horse is demonstrating a lovely 'square' halt. Its front legs and back legs are parallel as seen, and it is standing balanced and ready for another command.

secure position over the jump, and allows you to balance over the centre of gravity without putting pressure on the horse's back. Practise the 'jumping position' in walk, trot and canter before attempting to jump. Hold your weight out of the saddle (as for galloping), keeping the head up and hands forward. To practise the position required over the fence itself, halt the horse, and fold forwards from your hip joints with a flat back and chin up. Make sure that your lower legs stay in the correct position, neither too far back nor too far forward. Push your hands forwards slightly along the horse's neck without dropping the contact and without using the neck to balance yourself. Practise again until you can do it smoothly and without overbalancing.

Phases of the Jump

A horse's jump is divided into five phases:

- **Approach** The horse must be going forwards in balance, with plenty of impulsion and a good rhythm. This is the most important phase, and the one that usually determines how good the jump itself will be.
- **Take-off** The horse lowers its head and stretches its neck before take-off to assess the fence, and as it takes off it shortens its neck, raises its head and lifts off the ground, folding its forelegs beneath it. The horse's hocks come underneath it and, as its hind feet touch the ground, the horse stretches its head and neck, and uses its hindquarters to spring forwards and upwards.

▶ At take-off, the horse tucks in its forelegs.

◀ When jumping, the rider's hands should not press downwards on the neck, or be restrictive. Here the horse is jumping a cross pole.

- **Moment of suspension** The horse is stretched to its fullest in the air, with a rounded back.
- **Landing** The horse straightens its front legs, raises its head to balance itself and touches down with first its front, then its back, legs.
- **The getaway** The final phase should see the horse's hocks coming underneath it to rebalance and re-establish a good rhythm.

Starting to Jump

Start with trotting poles, to get you and the horse used to the idea of negotiating obstacles. These are heavy poles placed approximately 1.3–1.5 m (4 ft 3 in to 5 ft) apart for a horse; for a pony, place them approximately 1–1.35 m (3 ft 3 in to 4 ft 6 in) apart. They teach balance, rhythm and engagement, and help the rider to judge distances and 'get their eye in'. Use at least three poles to stop the horse jumping them in one go, and trot over them on each rein and from each direction. Do not canter over them unless you have increased the distances between them to account for the increase in stride length.

Add small jumps (cross-poles or uprights) into the grid, starting with two trotting poles and one jump at the end, until you and the horse are jumping a variety of obstacles in a straight line. Next, begin to build small courses, remembering to repeat each exercise on each rein to prevent the horse becoming one-sided.

Training a Young Horse

It is important that a horse's early education is done correctly. It is best left to those who know what they are doing; however, if you decide to train your young horse yourself, be sure to progress slowly, and take plenty of advice and help from experts.

▶ As the horse lands, his head and neck come upwards to balance himself – seen here after jumping an oxer fence.

Here are four golden rules to follow:

- Always be consistent and patient. Do not rush: horses like routine and need to have their confidence developed.
- Remember that young horses learn all the time. Make use of every opportunity to teach them about something new, and make sure that you never cut corners with their education.
- Try to imagine life as your horse sees it. It will help you to understand when and why it is frightened and will help you to anticipate how your horse will behave in certain situations.
- Remember that all horses need discipline: they will learn to take advantage if they can, and it is essential that they respect, but do not fear, you.

All horses are different, and will take different amounts of time to adjust to new situations and learn new things. You must be prepared to adapt your training regime to your horse, and do not panic if things take longer than you predicted.

Lungeing and Long-reining

- **Lungeing** can be used throughout a horse's active life as a method of training, or just for exercise. It teaches the horse to listen, to understand voice commands and to trust and obey the trainer. Done correctly, it will also increase concentration, strength and rhythm. It is a good way for a young horse to learn without the added problem of having to balance a rider on its back. Take care to lunge in big circles that do not put unnecessary pressure on its young joints, and do it for short periods of time. Voice commands must be simple and clear, and take time to make sure that your horse understands what you are asking.

- **Long-reining** is when a person walks behind the horse, controlling it by the use of two reins attached to the bit, then

▶ Lungeing is a valuable form of exercise for the horse. When lungeing, a good contact should be kept through the lunge line, as seen here.

taken through rings on the side of a roller. It is not easy to do well, but once mastered is an excellent way of getting the young horse to move forward confidently, and of developing the horse's outline, balance and understanding before it begins to be ridden. The horse can be schooled through all movements at all paces in the school, and asked to go out along lanes and tracks. Take care to make all commands clear, and remember that you are directly attached to the young horse's very sensitive mouth.

Starting to Ride

It is a good idea to work with an assistant in the beginning. Commence by riding in the school or a small area to allow you and your horse to get used to each other, and to the idea of riding. Gently teach the horse, using a light, firm aid, to start, stop, steer and turn. Do not ride tight circles or ask anything too ambitious too quickly.

As soon as it is safe to do so, start to hack out to maintain your horse's interest and forward thoughts. Try to get the horse used to hacking with a companion or on its own. And don't just slop along down the road: hacking is a great way to school the young horse. Introduce hillwork to help balance your horse and

◄ Start with riding at the school, before going out over wider areas.

► Hacking out gives the horse a break from schoolwork and helps to keep his interest. Hacking out with another horse will give a young horse confidence.

improve its fitness. Negotiate hazards whenever possible: open and close gates, walk down to the river, inspect that tractor on the side of the road, walk past those cows …

Practise 'schooling' (i.e. straight lines, bends and transitions) on tracks and in fields; your horse will learn that schooling is not something that only takes place in the confines of a school or arena.

Starting to Jump

The best way to teach a young horse to jump is to find small natural obstacles while out hacking. This takes away from the enormity of the occasion and lets the horse know that jumping is a perfectly usual thing to do and no fuss is to be made about it. Keep fences, whether outdoors or in a school environment, small and straightforward, and praise the horse when its completes the task successfully. Take care to give the horse all the help that you can; present it correctly and do not overface it.

Use your imagination when building fences; they do not have to cost the earth, and the greater variety the young horses sees the better. Make sure that you give it a chance to jump ditches, water and small combinations before you take it to a small competition. Hunting is an excellent way of introducing young horses to a variety of terrain and types of obstacles in a herd atmosphere.

Use every opportunity to socialize your horse and introduce it to new things and new occasions. Not only will it be fun for both of you, but also it will have the added benefit that, when you take your horse to its first event, it will take it all in its stride. It is important to stay calm and confident; never lose your temper or take it out on the horse. Remember that you are in charge, and be firm but sympathetic. Horses do not think like humans, and it is unfair to expect them to do what we want if we do not give them the correct signals.

▶ Lots of horses really enjoy jumping. Keep them interested by jumping different sorts of fences including show jumps and cross country fences.

Competing

Although winning should never be the be-all-and-end-all of why you ride, competing is, for many people, an enjoyable way of socializing with other people and horses, and a good way of checking that their riding and training are progressing in the right way. It is a good idea to try a variety of disciplines before you settle on one or two to do; consider what suits you and your horse, what you like the look of and what is practical.

Show Jumping

Show jumping, or stadium jumping, is a jumping class in which horses and riders negotiate a course of brightly coloured fences which are easily knocked down. Heights range from 'clear round' classes over fences 0.3 m (1 ft) high to the towering fences seen in international Grand Prix classes.

Equipment

Riders wear breeches, boots, either a shirt and tie or stock shirt and stock, a tweed, black or blue jacket, and a crash helmet that conforms to current safety standards. It is a good idea to wear gloves. Long hair should be neatly tied up or secured in a hairnet.

▶ The jumps in a show jumping course will all be different, some are brightly coloured and others quite creative. Most courses will include at least one combination of either two, or three jumps in a line and on a measured distance.

Horses should be presented looking their best, and usually wear forward-cut saddles specifically designed for show jumping. Most horses wear protective leg boots, often open-fronted tendon boots.

Rules

The course will include verticals, spreads, double and triple combinations, with turns and changes of direction appropriate to the level of competition. The purpose is to jump cleanly over a set course within an allotted time. Time faults are given for exceeding the time allowance. Jumping faults are incurred for knocking fences down and for refusals. Horses are allowed a limited number of refusals; either one or two, depending on the rules under which the class is judged, before being eliminated. A refusal can also lead to a rider going over the time allowed. Placings are based on the lowest number of faults accumulated. Those who jump clear in the first round of the competition usually have a jump-off over a raised and shortened course, and the course is timed; the fastest clear round over the jump-off course wins.

Competitors should walk the course carefully beforehand. This is a chance for the rider to walk the lines he or she will actually ride, finding the fastest and best possible paths.

◄ A low cross-pole jump is commonly used for beginner levels.

► Robert Smith is seen here jumping a large square oxer fence where the front and back of the jump are the same height, with a large spread in between.

Types of Jumps

- **Vertical** An upright fence made of poles or planks with no spread.
- **Filler** Not a type of fence, but a solid part below the poles, such as a gate, flower boxes or a roll-top.
- **Oxer** A spread fence, wider than a vertical. In essence, a vertical with a back pole added on a separate set of wings, in order to widen the distance jumped by the horse.
- **Square oxer** Both top poles are of an equal height.
- **Ascending oxer** The furthest pole is higher than the first.
- **Swedish oxer** The poles slant in opposite directions, so that they appear to form an X shape when seen head on.
- **Triple bar** A spread fence using three elements of graduating heights.
- **Wall** This type of jump is usually made to look like a brick wall, but the 'bricks' are constructed of a lightweight material and fall easily when knocked, so as not to damage the horse.
- **Hogsback** A type of jump where the tallest pole is in the centre.
- **Combination** Usually two or three jumps in a row, with no more than two strides between each. Two jumps in a row are called a 'double', and three jumps in a row are called a 'treble'. If a horse refuses the second or third element in one of these combinations, they must jump the whole combination again, not just the part they refused.
- **Fan** The rails on one side of the fence are spread out by degree, making the fence take the shape of a fan.
- **Open water** A wide ditch of water which a horse must jump cleanly.
- **Liverpool** A ditch or large tray of water under a vertical or oxer.

Principal Events

The principal international show-jumping events, held under the rules of the Fédération Equestre Internationale (FEI), are the Olympic Games, held every four years; the World

▶ Water jumps such as this one, which is called a Liverpool, are very wide and must be jumped cleanly. If the horse puts a foot in the water it is given penalty points.

Championships, also held every four years, on the 'even-numbered' years between Olympics; the annual World Cup; and continental championships, run every two years. Nations Cup competitions take place throughout the world several times a year. Each show-jumping nation also has a national championship.

Cross-Country

Cross-country is when riders and horses tackle a course of solid obstacles laid out in open country. A cross-country fence can be designed into almost any shape, and the higher up the levels a rider progresses, the more imaginative the designs become. Cross-country is the middle, and most influential, element of eventing, which is discussed later on.

Cross-Country Fences

These can include:

- **Arrowheads** These are narrow fences, shaped like triangles with the point towards the ground, designed to test accuracy and straightness.
- **Coffins** These are combination fences, consisting of an upright set of rails, with one or two strides to a ditch, then a further one or two strides to another set

◄ Most cross-country courses will include a water complex. This involves the horse jumping into and out of water over fences.

► Cross-country courses require both horse and rider to be very brave and skilled. The jumps can be very large, and because they are solid they do not knock down like show jumps.

of rails. The horse must approach the fence in a short, bouncy canter, in balance and in a good rhythm, and the rider must keep his or her riding strong and determined.

- **Corners** These are a V-shaped fence that can have an angle of up to 90 degrees, meant to be jumped on a line perpendicular to an imaginary bisecting line of the angle, as close to the narrowest point as possible. It is a great test of accuracy and requires precise riding, as there is no room for error.
- **Trakehners** The trakehner is a rail hanging over a ditch. Off-putting to both horse and rider, this is a test of boldness and bravery, and should be approached with energy and confidence.
- **Stone walls** Solid fences such as these are easy to jump, but require bold riding and bravery on the part of the horse.
- **Roll-tops** These are wooden fences with a rounded profile, which are forgiving and easy to jump.
- **Drops** The horse will not know that it is to land lower than its take-off spot, but the rider will, so it is up to the rider to make sure that the horse is well balanced with its weight on its hocks. The rider should lean back and slip the reins, but be ready to gather the horse up again on landing.
- **Steps and banks** These are tests of a horse's power and agility, and should be approached from a short, bouncy canter.
- **Open ditches** These are more intimidating to the rider than the horse, and the rider should therefore ride strongly and confidently, maintaining balance and rhythm, and remember to keep his or her head up and not to look down into the bottom of the ditch.

Hunter Trials

These are solely cross-country competitions, usually organized by riding clubs, Pony Clubs or hunts, and most often held in the spring or autumn. They take place in open fields, and competitors jump a course of wooden jumps usually of fairly basic design. The aim is to jump a clear round, and the winners are decided by several methods from those who jump clear, such as using a 'timed section'; this is part of the course, including jumps and perhaps a gate which must be undone and

▶ Jumps can include hedges. Jumps with a solid base and hedging on top are called 'brush fences'.

shut again, where riders have to go as fast as possible within the limits of safety. Some hunter trials are judged on style or, in the case of pairs classes, on how well each pair keeps together over the fences.

Equipment

Riders must wear a crash cap of approved standard and a body protector. Generally cross-country colours (a coloured rugby shirt and hat cover) are worn, but a plain sweatshirt and your standard hat cover are perfectly acceptable. It is a good idea to wear long sleeves to protect your arms, and never jump in anything but the correct footwear. Always remove all jewellery. Most people put protective over-reach and brushing boots on their horses' legs, and the saddle may be secured with an overgirth.

Dressage

Dressage is simply the correct training of horses. Any horse, from a Welsh Pony to a Thoroughbred, can do well, and dressage training will be of benefit to any horse undertaking any job. Competitive dressage, run internationally under the rules of the FEI but in individual countries by national governing bodies, is a way of

◄ Dressage arenas have letters along their sides and ends. During dressage tests, letters such as the K seen here indicate where movements should take place.

► Dressage is a sport that can be enjoyed by any aged rider and any type of horse or pony. Dressage competitions cater for a full range of abilities from starter level to the very top.

testing that you and your horse are training along the right lines. Affiliated dressage starts at preliminary level and continues through to Grand Prix. Dressage also forms the first part of the three-day event.

The Arena

There are two sizes of arena: 20 m x 40 m (66 ft x 132 ft) and 20 m x 60 m (66 ft x 198 ft). The smaller arena is used for the lower levels of both pure and eventing dressage, while the 'long' arena is used at the more advanced competitions.

The letters along the sides of the arena indicate where movements should take place. In the short arena, the letters, commencing clockwise at A, run A-F-B-M-C-H-E-K, with D, X and G on the centre line. The letters in the long arena are A-F-P-B-R-M-C-H-S-E-V-K, with D-L-X-I-G on the centre line. X always marks the centre of the arena. At the start of the test, the horse enters at A and progresses down the centre line. The judge sits at C; as a rider progresses up the levels, there will also be judges at up to four other letters: B, E, M and H.

Scales of Training

The training scale is used as a guide for the correct training of the dressage horse. It is not meant to be a rigid format, but a series of 'building blocks' with which to progress. Each element is interconnected. First defined in Germany, their German meanings are more encom-passing and comprehensive than the words in English. The six scales are:

- Relaxation (*Losgelassenheit*)
- Rhythm and regularity (*Takt*)
- Contact (*Anlehnung*)
- Impulsion (*Schwung*)
- Straightness (*Geraderichtung*)
- Collection (*Versammlung*)

▶ Turnout is very important in dressage. Manes are plaited to create clean, long lines, while tails are left unplaited, though they will be trimmed and thinned.

Equipment

At lower levels, riders wear tweed, black or blue coats with a shirt and tie or stock and stock shirt, and either a crash cap or hunting cap, although the former is recommended for safety. At advanced competitions, a tailcoat with a yellow waistcoat and top hat is correct.

Horses are not permitted to wear boots or bandages, or training aids such as martingales. Novice horses wear snaffle bridles, and advanced horses compete in double bridles. Dressage saddles, designed to help the rider to adopt the correct position and with straight flaps to avoid hindering the horse's movement, are used – although beginners would be advised to start in a general-purpose saddle rather than buy an expensive dressage saddle that they may not use again. Horses have plaited manes, but their tails are usually left unplaited. Turnout is very important.

Principal Events

The Olympics, World Championships and continental championships run in a four-year cycle. At these, team medals are contested first, and all four team members ride the Grand Prix test, which is divided into two parts on consecutive days. The three best scores from each nation are totalled to count for the final team score. From 2008, the Olympic teams will consist of only three riders, so all three scores will count. The scoreboard is then wiped clean, and the top 25 riders from the team competition go on to perform the Grand Prix Special, battling for gold, silver and bronze individual medals. The top 15 from this then go on to a further competition for another set of medals for the Grand Prix Freestyle (*Kür*), which is performed to music of the riders' choice.

Eventing

Eventing is possibly the ultimate test of horse and rider. The competitor is expected to

▶ This elegant combination of horse and rider are competing in a top level competition. The rider is wearing the top hat and tails required for this level of competition.

complete a dressage test, cross-country round and show-jumping round, so must be proficient in all three phases and prove boldness, accuracy, suppleness, trainability and stamina.

One-Day Events

At affiliated level, each country's national body runs one-day events, where all three elements take place on the same day, at a variety of levels. Many Pony Clubs and riding clubs also run unaffiliated one-day events at novice and open standard, and horse and rider comb-inations should be proficient at these before attempting affiliated competition. You will be given set times by the organizers at which you must do each phase; there will usually be an hour or more between each one. The dressage is always performed first, then the show jumping and finally the cross-country, although the last two phases are sometimes swapped around. It is important to leave yourself enough time to walk the show jumping and cross-country courses thoroughly, and work out your approach to each fence.

Between phases, cool your horse down, untack the horse if appropriate, and make sure that it is comfortable. It is unwise to leave your horse tied to the back of the lorry (truck) or trailer if you are not in attendance, in case it breaks free. Leave yourself enough time to warm up correctly for each phase; it is no fun to be in a hurry and you will not perform to your best. After the cross-country, dismount after crossing the finishing line, loosen the girth and walk the horse back to the lorry. Wash the horse down thoroughly to cool it and remove sweat, and walk it until its heart rate has returned to normal. Check the horse carefully for any lumps, bumps and cuts that it might have picked up across country, and let it drink – but do not let it drink too much too quickly because it might develop colic.

Three-Day Events

These are run under the auspices of the FEI, which is the governing body of all horse sports internationally. They start at CCI* level,

▶ Eventing is mentally and physically challenging for horse and rider because it includes dressage, as seen here, show-jumping and cross-country phases, requiring a versatile and well trained horse.

and the top level is CCI****. There are six CCI**** events in the world each year: Badminton and Burghley in Britain, Kentucky in the United States, Luhmuhlen in Germany, Pau in France and Adelaide in Australia. Although they are called three-day events, the competitions actually take five days from start to finish. The first veterinary inspection, where the horses are trotted up in front of the ground jury (panel of judges) for soundness, takes place on Wednesday. There are then two days of dressage on Thursday and Friday. The cross-country phase is completed on Saturday, and the show jumping, preceded by a final veterinary inspection and trot-up, finishes the event on Sunday.

A three-day event is very demanding for horse and rider, and both must be in peak physical condition. Until recently, Saturday's cross-country phase was termed the speed and endurance section. Riders and horses first completed a short section of 'roads and tracks', to be completed in trot in a certain time, then galloped round a steeplechase course, then underwent a short section of roads and tracks, which led

then to the 10-minute box. Here horses were washed and cooled down, and inspected by the vet during a 10-minute interval, then they set out on a tough cross-country track of several miles. Almost all events have now adopted the shortened version of a three-day event, however, which does not include roads and tracks, or steeplechase. Riders must be sure therefore that they have warmed their horses up sufficiently to undergo

◄ It is important to keep the horse cool between phases at an event. At the top events, and in hot climates, fans such as these, which are blowing a fine mist of cool water might be used to keep the horse cool.

► The cross-country phase of eventing is usually last on one-day events, or second on three-day events. All riders must walk all courses before riding them, to assess angles and distances.

such a demanding test without these elements, which were in effect preparation for cross-country, and be sure that their horses are fit enough to complete the course without distress.

Showing, Gymkhanas and Other Events

There are a multitude of activities that you can do with your horse, either competitively (such as showing, endurance riding, team-chasing or driving) or non-competitively (such as fun rides and hunting). The only important thing is to find something that both you and your horse enjoy and are suited to, and the best way to do this is to try a range of different options.

Competing is a good way of measuring the progress you are making as a rider and as a trainer of your horse, and it is a good incentive to improve, but it should not become all-important and you must be realistic in your expectations.

The key to all success is preparation. Practise at home what must be done in the show ring, and make sure that your tack, horse and clothing are clean and ready the night before. Get there in plenty of time, and check whether things are running to order before you get your horse out of the lorry (truck) or trailer. Leave enough time to dress, warm up and have a final polish before your class; if entering more than one class, ensure that they do not clash.

Showing

'Showing' is a very broad term, but basically covers classes judged on conformation, way of going, turnout and paces. At the top end, your horse will have to be a beautifully behaved runway model with exceptional

▶ It is important for the horse and rider to practise at home and be prepared physically and mentally for competitions. Also make sure that tack, horse and clothing are ready the night before.

presence, but there are lots of local shows with classes for all sorts. Some are for specific breeds or types, such as native ponies or coloured horses; others are judged on suitability, jumping, turnout or simply the pony the judge would most like to take home. Working hunter classes will require you to jump a round over rustic fences, then those who complete this successfully will be asked to come back into the ring and perform a show.

There are also many in-hand classes where the horses are not ridden, but shown by someone on the ground. These may be a good starting point if you have nerves about riding in front of other people. All young stock and breeding stock are shown in-hand, and there are classes for almost all types of horse in-hand at many shows.

Usually, all competitors walk, trot and canter around as a group in ridden classes, then are asked to give short individual shows. The judge may then ask to see the horses or ponies without their saddles and trotted up in front of them, and will then pick a winner. Remember that showing is subjective; what one judge likes another will not, and it is best to shrug your shoulders and plan for another day if things do not go to plan.

Turnout is very important, and horses should be as clean and tidy as you can manage. Your appearance is

◄ Before you get your horse out of the trailer, check that the event is running to order.

► By having a panel of several judges, as seen at this jumping competition, there is no room for error. They are well placed in the ring to evaluate each individual competitor.

important, too; find out the correct attire for the class you are entering, and make sure that you are spotless and neat. Most classes will require horses and ponies to be plaited; however, classes for native ponies and Arabs do not.

Gymkhana

Gymkhana games are often offered at local shows and Pony Club events, and consist of a series of races while carrying out different activities. Some popular ones include:

- Bending race
- Egg-and-spoon race
- Walk, trot and canter
- Ride and run
- Apple bobbing
- Sack race
- Cup race
- Flag race

Fast, nippy ponies are best suited to these, but there is no reason why the average horse should not give them a go, provided the rider continues to ride well and not get carried away in the heat of the moment into wrenching the mount's head around, walloping the horse or generally riding badly.

◄ ► There are many different types of gymkhana games, but for all of them the pony and rider have to be very athletic and quick.

Endurance

Endurance riding is long-distance riding over various types of terrain. This can be a very rewarding sport for those who do not wish to show or jump their horses, and is known for its friendliness and approachability at the lower levels. Arab horses are particularly well suited to it because of their great stamina, but any type of horse can do well. Rides start at just a few miles in distance, but progress up the grades to international competitions, which can be as much as 160 km (100 miles) in a single day, and many more over several days. Fitness of both horse and rider is crucial, and there are well-regulated veterinary inspections.

Hunting

Hunting has always been an excellent training ground for horse and rider, and great fun for them both as well. It teaches horses to cross different terrain and jump a variety of obstacles in company, and is a good way of getting young, inexperienced horses socialized and going forwards. It is never compulsory to jump, and there are many hunts who jump little or not at all. Contact your local pack for more details and to ask whether you may come out. Horses should wear clean, well-fitting tack, and riders should be neat and tidy. Remember that you will be in the saddle for a long time, and it is important to be warm and comfortable.

Fun Rides

These are organized by local hunts, Pony Clubs or riding clubs, and consist of riding in groups or alone

◄ Arabian horses such as these are particularly well suited to endurance riding since they naturally have great stamina and are very tough.

► Endurance riding can be rewarding in its variety of terrain.

round a preset course, which will often include optional jumps. They are an enjoyable, relaxed way of getting used to riding in public and a way to educate your horse about how to behave with other horses without the pressure of competition.

Competition Checklist

If you go to a competition or other outing with your horse, you will need some of the following items, depending on the type of event in which you are taking part. It is better to take too much than too little, and you will soon know what is necessary and what is not.

Horse

- Saddle and numnah (saddle pad)
- Stirrups and stirrup leathers
- Girth
- Martingale/breastplate if worn
- Basic first-aid kit, including your vet's telephone number
- Plaiting bands/needle and thread
- Grooming kit: dandy brush, body brush, curry comb, hoof pick, stable rubber, hoof oil and brush, mane comb
- Two buckets: one for washing and one for your horse to drink from
- Sponges and sweat scraper
- Sweat rug and surcingle
- Travelling boots
- Tail bandage
- Headcollar and rope
- Water carrier and lots of water

▶ Western show classes require slightly different attire than English ones. Here the handler and horse are beautifully presented for a 'halter' class in western showing.

For jumping

- Brushing boots, over-reach boots, bandages and gamgee tissue
- Studs and tools to put them in and take them out
- Cross-country surcingle
- Tape for boots, to make sure they will not come off mid-round

Rider

- Approved standard hat
- Jacket
- Shirt and tie, or stock shirt, stock and stock pins
- Light-coloured breeches or jodhpurs
- Boots, or jodhpur boots and half-chaps
- Hairnet
- Basic human first-aid kit
- Whip/spurs as required
- Gloves
- Body protector
- Cross-country shirt and cap cover
- Waterproof clothing for wet conditions and sunscreen for hot days

▶ Fun rides are a great way to get your horse used to being around other horses.

Useful Addresses

British Horse Society
Abbey Park
Stareton
Kenilworth
Warwickshire, CV8 2XZ
UK
Tel: +44 (0)2476 840500
www.bhs.org.uk

**The Association of British
Riding Schools**
Unit 8, Bramble Hill Farm
Five Oaks Road
Slinfold, Horsham
West Sussx RH13 0RL
UK
Tel: +44 (0)1403 790294
www.abrs-info.org

British Dressage
Meriden Business Park
Copse Drive
Meriden, West Midlands
CV5 9RG
UK
Tel: +44 (0)2476 698830
www.britishdressage.co.uk

**British Show Jumping
Association**
Meriden Business Park
Copse Drive
Meriden, West Midlands
CV5 9RG
UK
Tel: +44 (0)2476 8800
www.bsja.co.uk

British Eventing
Stoneleigh Park
Kenilworth
Warwickshire, CV8 2RN
UK
Tel: +44 (0)845 2623344
www.britisheventing.com

British Equine Veterinary Association
Mulberry House
31 Market Street
Fordham, Ely
Cambridgeshire, CB7 5LQ
UK
Tel: + 44 (0)1638 723 555
www.beva.org.uk

Rare Breeds Survival
Stoneleigh Park
Kenilworth
Warwickshire, CV8 2LG
UK
Tel: +44 (0)2476 696 551
www.rbst.org.uk

American Association of
Equine Practitioners
4075 Iron Works Parkway
Lexington
Kentucky 40511
USA
Tel: +1 859 233 0147
www.aaep.org

American Association of
Riding Schools
8375 Coldwater Road
Davison
Michigan 48423-8966
USA
Tel: +1 810 496 0360
www.ucanride.com

United States Dressage Federation
4047 Iron Works Parkway
Lexington
Kentucky 40511
USA
Tel: +1 859 971 7722
www.usdf.org

United States Equestrian Federation
4047 Iron Works Parkway
Lexington
Kentucky 405 I I
USA
Tel: +1 859 258 2472
www.usef.org

United States Eventing Association
525 Old Waterford Road, NW
Leesburg
Virginia 20176
USA
Tel: +1 703 779 0440
www.useventing.com

Publications:

Horse & Hound
9th Floor Blue Fin Building
110 Southwark Street
London, SE1 0SU, UK
Tel: +44 (0)20 3148 4562
www.horseandhound.co.uk

Equine Journal
83 Leicester Street
North Oxford
Massachusetts 01537
USA
Tel: +1 508 987 5886
www.equinejournal.com

Further Reading

Baskett, John, *The Horse in Art*, Yale University Press (New Haven, Conneticut), 2006

Bowen, Edward, *Horse Racing's Greatest Moments*, Eclipse Press (Lexington, Kentucky), 2001

Burn, D. and Fitzsimons, C., *Identification Guide: Horses & Ponies*, Flame Tree Publishing (London, UK), 2008

Draper, Judith, *The Ultimate Encyclopedia of Horse Breeds and Horse Care*, Hermes House (London, UK), 2003

Draper, Judith, *The Book of Horses: An Encyclopedia of Horse Breeds of the World*, Southwater Publishing (London, UK), 2003

Johns, Catherine, *Horses: History, Myth, Art*, Harvard University Press (Cambridge, Massachusetts), 2007

Frape, David, *Equine Nutrition and Feeding*, Wiley-Blackwell (Hoboken, New Jersey), 2004

Giffin, James M. and Gore, Tom, *Horse Owner's Veterinary Handbook*, Howell Book House (Hoboken, New Jersey), 1997

Green, John, *Horse Anatomy*, Dover Publications (Mineola, New Jersey), 2006

Hakola, Susan E., *The Equus Illustrated Handbook of Equine Anatomy*, Primedia Equine Network (Gaithersburg, Maryland), 2006

Harris, Susan E., *Horse Gaits, Balance and Movement*, Howell Book House (Hoboken, New Jersey), 2005

Harris, Susan E., *Grooming to Win: How to Groom, Trim, Braid and Prepare Your Horse for Show*, Howell Book House (Hoboken, New Jersey), 1991

Hausman, Gerald and Hausman, Loretta, *The Mythology of Horses: Horse Legend and Lore Throughout the Ages*, Three Rivers Press (New York, New York), 2003

Hedge, Juliet and Wagoner, Don (Ed.s), *Horse Conformation: Structure, Soundness and Performance*, The Lyons Press (Guilford, Conneticut), 2004

Hendricks, Bonnie L., *International Encyclopedia of Horse Breeds*, University of Oklahoma Press (Norman, Oklahoma), 2007

Hill, Cherry, *Horse Handling & Grooming*, Storey Publishing (North Adams, Massachusetts), 1997

Jahiel, Jessica, *The Rider's Problem Solver*, Storey Publishing (North Adams, Massachusetts), 2006

Lewis, Lon D.; Knight, Anthony; Lewis, Bart; and Lewis, Corey, *Feeding and Care of the Horse*, Wiley-Blackwell (Hoboken, New Jersey), 1996

Lucas, Sharon, *The New Encyclopedia of the Horse*, Dorling Kindersley (London, UK), 2001

McBane, Susan, *The Illustrated Encyclopedia of Horse Breeds*, Wellfleet Press (Seacaucus, New Jersey), 1997

Micklem, William, *Complete Horse Riding Manual*, Dorling Kindersley (London, UK), 2003

Murdoch, Wendy, *Simplify Your Riding*, Carriage House Publishing (Middleton, New Hampshire), 2004

Pavord, Tony and Pavord, Marcy, *The Complete Equine Veterinary Manual*, David & Charles Publishers (Newton Abbot, Devon, UK), 2004

Pickeral, Tamsin, *The Horse: 30,000 Years of the Horse in Art*, Merrell Publishers (London, UK), 2006

Self-Bucklin, Gincy, *How Your Horse Wants You to Ride*, Howell Book House (Hoboken, New Jersey), 2006

Sly, Debby, *The Ultimate Book of the Horse and Rider*, Hermes House (London, UK), 2004

Smith, Mike, *Getting the Most from Riding Lessons*, Storey Publishing (North Adams, Massachusetts), 1998

Swinney, Nicola Jane, *Horse Breeds of the World*, The Lyons Press (Guilford, Conneticut), 2006

Vogel, Colin, *Complete Horse Care Manual*, Dorling Kindersley (London, UK), 2003

Glossary

Action The way a horse moves at various gaits, also reflected in head, neck and tail carriage.

Aids Signals from the rider or handler to the horse that imparts to the animal what the rider/handler wants it to do. They can be natural (such as mind, seat, weight, body) or artificial (such as whips and spurs).

Airs Movements of the High School (*Haute École*), associated with advanced or classical equitation, such as 'airs above the ground', where the horse leaves the ground.

Appendicular skeleton Bones in horse's legs, shoulders and hindquarters.

Axial skeleton Skull, backbone and ribcage.

Back at the knee A conformational fault in which the forelegs curve back below the knee. Opposite of over at the knee.

Bay Brown horse with black points.

Brand Marks put on horse's coat for identification.

Breed (n.) Subspecies of horse that has a defined set of distinguishing characteristics, which may have been encouraged and developed by man.

Blaze Wide white mark on horse's face.

Bone Measured round the circumference of the horse's leg, just below the knee. Dictates how much weight the horse can carry. Hard bone is desirable as it enables horses to carry heavier weights.

Bowed hocks Hocks turn out, with feet turning in. *See also* 'cow hocks'; 'sickle hocks'.

Buckskin Colour similar to dun, but generally brighter and darker; the colour of a tanned hide.

Bull neck Short, thick neck.

Calf knees Also known as 'back at the knee'.

Canines Four teeth in the interdental space, usually found only in male horses (also called 'tushes').

Cardiac sphincter Muscle at entrance to horse's stomach.

Carriage driving Driving a two- or four-wheeled carriage using one, two or four horses. Modern carriage driving trials are three day events.

Carriage horse Horse used to pull carriages – usually relatively light and elegant and used in carriage driving competition.

Carthorse Large, strong, cold-blooded draught horse used for pulling carts or other heavy loads.

Chestnut Horse with an orange or reddish brown coat, of varying shades.

Coach horse Horse used to pull a coach or carriage, usually powerfully built for fairly heavy loads.

Cob Small, stocky horses with compact bodies, short legs and steady dispositions. A type, rather than a breed, usually of unknown or mixed breeding.

Coffin joint Between pedal bone and short pastern in horse's foot.

Coldblood (n.), cold-blooded (adj.) Large horse with calm, gentle disposition; suitable for slow, hard work. Draught horses are considered coldbloods.

Colt Uncastrated male horse or pony under the age of four.

Conformation A horses' shape and 'composition'; particularly determined by the body parts' proportion and relationship to one another.

Coronet band At the top of horse's foot.

Cow hocks Hocks turn in, with feet turning out. *See also* 'bowed hocks'; 'sickle hocks'.

Croup Topline of a horse measured from the point of the hip to the point of the buttock.

Dam The horse's female parent.

Depth of girth The measurement from the horse's withers to the elbow.

Dental star Black mark found on front of tables of teeth.

Destrier This word described the finest and strongest medieval warhorse ridden by knights. A type of horse, rather than a breed.

Digital cushion Large piece of tissue at back of horse's foot (also called 'plantar cushion').

Dished face A concave profile, such as that of the Arabian.

Dock The part of the horse's tail on which the hair grows.

Dorsal stripe A line of darker hair extending from the horse's neck to the tail, seen in the 'primitive' breeds. Also called 'eel stripe'.

Draught Heavy horse, or a term applied to a horse drawing any vehicle.

Dressage Training a horse to the highest possible level, so that it accurately performs a number of movements at different paces in a relaxed way in response to the rider's subtle aids.

Dun Horse with a yellowy brown coat and black points, often with a dorsal stripe.

Endocrine system Releases hormones into horse's body.

English saddle Saddle with a steel cantle and pommel and no horn (unlike a Western saddle), designed to allow freedom of movement.

Ermine marks Patches of colour in horse's white socks or stockings.

Eventing Eventing is a complete competition combining dressage, show jumping and cross-country. Events take place over one, two or three days.

Ewe neck Well-developed muscle underneath the neck and weak topline.

Feather Long hair on the lower legs and fetlocks, common in heavy draught breeds.

Flaxen White mane and tail on chestnut.

Filly Female horse or pony under the age of four.

Five-gaited A horse that can demonstrate five gaits, three natural (walk, trot, canter) and two 'man-made' (slow and rack).

Freezemark White numbers on horse's coat, put on with chilled markers, for identification.

Frog Horny, V-shaped part of bottom of horse's foot.

Gait The horse's action, such as walk, trot or canter; also applied to the American gaited horses.

Gaited horse Horse that performs a foot fall pattern outside the normal walk, trot, canter sequence.

Galvayne's Groove Develops down the outside of upper corner incisors; can be used to help with judging a horse's age.

Gelding Castrated male horse.

Goose-rump When the quarters slope sharply from croup to dock.

Hack General riding horse. Show quality hacks have flawless manners and looks.

Hand Traditional unit of measurement for horses. One hand equals 4 in (10.16 cm). The symbol for this unit is 'hh' (standing for 'hands high').

Harness horse Horse used for pulling vehicles.

Haute École High School, the classical art of advanced riding, seen, for example, in the Spanish Riding School of Vienna.

Heavy horse Any large draught breed.

Herring-gutted When the underside of the body slopes steeply upwards towards the stifle.

Hindquarters The back quarters of a horse, from the flank to the tail.

Hollow back Dipped back; can develop with age. Also called 'sway back'.

Hotblood (n.), hot-blooded (adj.) Light saddle horse such as the Thoroughbred and the Arabian, with highly-strung, fiery-tempered nature.

Hunter Horse bred and trained to be ridden for hunting. Can either be show hunters, or working/field hunters.

Incisors The 12 biting teeth at front of a horse's mouth.

Infundibulum Large dark hole found in centre of tables of teeth.

Interdental space Gap between the incisors and premolars.

Jibbah A shield-shaped bulge on the forehead, unique to the Arabian.

Isabella Another term for palomino.

Jumper's bump When the horse has a pronounced croup.

Laminae Leaves of tissue between hoof wall and pedal bone.

Light horse Any equine over 15 hh that is not one of the heavy draught breeds.

Light of bone A conformation fault where the amount of bone below the knee is too small in comparison to the size of the horse.

Loaded shoulder Excessive muscle formation; a conformational fault.

Lungeing (Also called 'lunging' or 'longeing'). Where a horse is held on a long rope and made to circle round its trainer for training and exercise.

Lymphatic system Drains excess fluid and helps horse's body to fight infection.

Mare Adult female horse or pony.

Mealy muzzle Oatmeal-coloured muzzle seen on the Exmoor Pony.

Mitbah The angle at which the Arabian's head meets the neck; unique to the breed.

Molars The 12 chewing teeth at back of a horse's mouth.

Navicular bone Small bone in horse's foot.

Over at the knee A conformational fault; the opposite of back at the knee.

Pacer A horse that performs a lateral action, rather than diagonal like the trot.

Palomino Horse with a yellowy gold coat and white mane and tail.

Pastern bone Extends from horse's lower leg into top of the foot.

Pedal bone Large bone in horse's foot.

Perlino Cream-coloured horse with blue eyes.

Piebald Horse with black-and-white patches.

Pigeon toes When the toes turn in.

Plantar cushion Large piece of tissue at back of horse's foot (also called 'digital cushion').

Points of the horse Specific external parts of the horse. In relation to colour, the points of the horse refer to the mane, tail, muzzle, tips of the ears and lower legs.

Polo pony Fast, agile and quick-thinking horse used to play the game of polo, even if it is taller then the maximum height for a pony (14.2 hands).

Pony Small horse, usually under 14.2 hands. However, ponies are not necessarily simply a small or miniature horse as they tend to differ from horses in other ways. For example they may have thicker manes, tails and coat; proportionally shorter legs, wider barrels, shorter and thicker necks; and sometimes calmer temperaments.

Posting In rising trot, when the rider rises from the saddle for one beat and sits in the saddle for the alternate beat.

Premolars The 12 chewing teeth at back of a horse's mouth.

Prepotency The ability to pass on characteristics to the progeny.

Presence The 'sparkle' seen in show horses and competition horses that says, 'Look at me.'

Primitive The term used to describe the early horse breeds, such as Przewalski's, Tarpan and Solutre.

Prophet's thumb mark Muscular indentation, usually on neck or shoulder; considered lucky.

Quarters See hindquarters.

Rack A four-beat gait known as the fifth gait in some North American breeds. Also called 'single-foot'.

Remount A horse used for service in an army or the police force.

Roach back Back curves upwards towards and over loins.

Roman nose Nose that is convex in profile.

Saddle horse Horse bred or trained for riding.

Sickle hocks Hocks that are too bent and weak. See also 'bowed hocks'; 'cow hocks'.

Sire The horse's male parent.

Skewbald Horse with patches of white and any colour other than black.

Snip White on horse's nose.

Sock White on a horse's leg extending from the foot to the fetlock or below.

Sole Bottom of horse's foot.

Sport horse Type of horse – purebred or crossbred – that is used for equestrian disciplines such as dressage, jumping, eventing or endurance.

Stallion Adult male horse that has not been castrated (gelded).

Star White mark on forehead or between eyes.

Stocking White on horse's leg extending from the foot to between the fetlock and knee or hock (or sometimes higher, known as 'white legs').

Stripe Narrow white mark on horse's face.

Studbook Book in which the pedigree of purebred stock are officially recorded.

Swan neck Long neck which is dipped in front of the withers, then arched, with the highest point further back, then the poll.

Sway back Dipped back; can develop with age. Also called 'hollow back'.

Tables Top surface of lower incisors.

Tack The various saddles, bridles and other equipment used in horse riding, driving and management.

Teaser A substitute stallion used to test whether a mare is ready to be mated.

Tölt The lateral gait seen in the Icelandic Horse.

Trotting horse; trotter Horse that has been trained to trot, for example in harness racing.

Tushes Four teeth in the interdental space, usually found only in male horses (also called 'canines').

Type 'Types' of horses are not breeds, but usually a group of breeds that share similar characteristics or are used for a particular activity such as polo or hunting.

Wall Outside of horse's foot.

Warmblood (n.), warm-blooded (adj.) Generally, a half-bred or part-bred horse of an even temperament, usually crossed out from Arabian or Thoroughbred stock, or the result of a cross between hot-blooded and cold-blooded breeds to create a sturdy, athletic horse.

Western pleasure Western-style competition, in particular judging conformation and temperament, gait cadence and speed.

Western saddle Saddle used for western riding and for working on horse and cattle ranches, a distinctive feature of which is the horn.

Withers The highest part of a horse's back, on the ridge behind the neck and between the shoulders.

White face When the white on a horse's face covers the eyes, forehead and much of the muzzle.

Whorls Places where the hair swirls and grows in different directions.

Wolf teeth Remnants of defunct first premolars; one or more found in some horses.

Zebra stripes Dark stripes on the horse's lower legs, a primitive feature.

Index